Get Unstuck for Kids!

A Fun, Interactive Guide to Empower Your Child for Life!

By
#1 Best-selling Authors

John Seeley M.A.
&
Amanda van der Gulik

John Seeley M.A. & Amanda van der Gulik

Get Unstuck for Kids!

John Seeley M.A. & Amanda van der Gulik

Get Unstuck for Kids! – John Seeley M.A. & Amanda van der Gulik
©2014 Published by Heart Fire Press

EDITORIAL OFFICE:
Blue Moon Wonders
4492 Camino de la Plaza Suite 564
San Diego, CA 92173

Editorial and production: Bob Adams
Type design and typography: Sam Johnson
Formatting by Claudia Suzanne
Cover design: Karen Floyd, San Diego, CA
Cover photo By Larry Silva, c. 2014

All rights reserved. This book may not be reproduced in whole Or in part, or transmitted in any form- or by any means electronic, mechanical photocopying, recording, or other, without written permission from the publisher, except by a reviewer who may quote brief passages in a review.

Library of Congress Cataloguing-in-Publication Data

Seeley, John Herbert, Amanda van der Gulik
Get Unstuck for Kids! / John Herbert Seeley, Amanda van der Gulik

ISBN: 978 0 9765942-5-3

Printed in the USA on acid-free paper
Distributed by Blue Moon Wonders

10 9 8 7 6 5 4 3 2 1

All Rights Reserved. No part of this publication may be reproduced in any form or by any means, including scanning, photocopying, or otherwise without prior written permission of the copyright holder.

Copyright © 2014

Manufactured in the United State

This book is dedicated to all kids
who choose to be empowered
and to all parents who wish to
empower their children.

John Seeley M.A. & Amanda van der Gulik

Welcome!

We've put together this book for you to help you with getting your own child 'unstuck' in his or her life. You may find that the messages, stories, and activities are also helpful for yourself.

The way to best use this book is to read the chapters for yourself and implement the lessons into your own life, thereby role modeling what you want your child to learn. At the end of each chapter you will find a story that compliments the theme of each chapter. These stories are meant for you to read to your child as an easy means for you to pass along the messages in that chapter. You'll find questions and exercises after each story to help you get your child to work the topic more deeply into their subconscious mind.

The goal of this book is to give you, the parent, the tools that you need to help empower your child so that he or she will live a happy life full of self-worth and the tools to deal with their negative setbacks that we all experience in our lives.

We are not child doctors and do not claim that the theory, stories, exercises and activities in this book will indeed absolutely help your child to become 'unstuck' in their lives. These exercises and suggestions are presented to your child because either John, or Amanda or both have used each one successfully in their own lives and in the lives of Amanda's children. We will not accept responsibility if these exercises do not help your child or if they harm in any way.

John Seeley M.A. & Amanda van der Gulik

John Seeley M.A. & Amanda van der Gulik

Table of Contents

Welcome! vii

1   Changing the Life of Your Child 1
     Story: 6
     Scotty Learns About "THE PERFECT DAY" 6
         Activity 1 13
         Activity 2 14
         Activity 3 16

2   There is a Way Out for Your Child 17
     Story: James Finds His Inner Voice 21
         Activity 1 27
         Activity 2 28
         Activity 3 29
     Autobiography in Five Short Chapters by Portia Nelson
     29

3   Miracles Happen Every Day 31
     Story: Not Such a PERFECT DAY for Scottie 34
         Activity 1 38
         Activity 2: 39
         Activity 3 39

| 4 | Growth vs. Decay | 41 |

Story: Lucy Learns a Hard Lesson about Asking For Help 44

- Activity 1 50
- Activity 2 51
- Activity 3 52

| 5 | Your and Your Child's Word | 53 |

Story: Jeannie Doesn't Keep Her Word 57

- Activity 1 60
- Activity 2 61
- Activity 3 62

| 6 | Fear vs. Desire | 63 |

Story: Scottie's PERFECT DAY Finally Arrives 68

- Activity 1 77
- Activity 2 78
- Activity 3 80

| 7 | How to Change Your Child's Mind | 81 |

Story: Annie Gets Something Even Better Than What She Wants 85

- Activity 1 94
- Activity 2 95
- Activity 3 96

8	Helping Your Child to Take Back Their Power	97
	Story: Nat Conquers Her Fear	101
	Activity 1	108
	Activity 2	109
	Activity 3	110
9	Forgiveness	111
	Soul Letters: Seven Steps to Truth	115
	Story: Lucy Learns To Forgive	117
	Activity 1	127
	Activity 2	128
	Activity 3	130
10	Commitment	131
	Story:	134
	Scottie Creates His First Vision Board	134
	Activity 1	141
	Activity 2	143
	Activity 3	144
11	Gratitude	145
	Story: Jessie Learns About Gratitude	148
	Activity 1	155
	Activity 2	157
	Activity 3	158

| 12 | Your Child's Next Step | 159 |

Story: Scottie Finally Gets What He Wants 164

    Activity 1 165

    Activity 2 166

    Activity 3 167

Other Titles by John & Amanda 168

    John Seeley M. A. 168

    Amanda van der Gulik 169

    Resource Suggestions 169

1   Changing the Life of Your Child

*"Insanity: doing the same thing over and over again,
expecting different results."
Albert Einstein*

Change happens instantly. Deciding to change takes some time. When you can see that your child's life is not going the right way, then you will know that it is time to change. Even though you will know that change will be a good thing for your child, be prepared for your child to resist the change. It's not because he doesn't want a new way of life, it's because he knows the old way and it feels comfortable and familiar to him. It's not the life that he really wants but he also knows that it's not the worst that could happen to him. You will need to be patient and persistent. He may truly want to make a change but simply doesn't know how to do it. You can be his coach, his cheerleader so to speak.

Your child may truly feel like he is stuck in a rut. This is the time when you really need to encourage him to reach out for the help he so desperately needs. He may come to a place of frustration and hopelessness and these are your signs to take certain action to encourage him to get the help that he needs. Reinforcement may be needed here. Sometimes we can feel that to ask for help is a sign of failure. But it is NOT! You need to make sure that he understands that to move ahead, he will need to accept that there is help for him. That he is not alone.

You need to show him that asking for help is the absolute best thing he can do for himself.

Ever feel like you don't deserve help or that there is simply no hope for you? Well, that's what he may be feeling right now, and that's when he MUST reach out! I've included a story for you that you can read together with your child to show him what you want to convey so that it is coming from a third party, which can sometimes be helpful. It's very true that those nearest and dearest to us will often not accept our help, but they may listen to someone else. I know it can be frustrating and that's why we are here to help you with this book.

There is always help available for your child, but he may just be too close to the problem to see it. He may think he can really see his situation accurately and that there really is no way out, but his conclusion is WRONG! There is always help. He matters! Once you can help him to see this, and be willing to accept help, he will be able to find a way out.

Sometimes we take certain experiences to mean that we are not good enough. For example, John was fired twice in six months and took that to mean that he was simply "not good enough" when in reality he was, he just needed to find a better place for himself. We get so misguided by thinking that other people's opinions of us matter more than our own. That is simply not true. For each of us, our own opinions matter more than anyone else's. This is your life, not someone else's. Their opinions matter for their lives, not yours. I once heard someone once say the following message, I can't remember anymore who it was, but the message has stayed with me to this day and I have found it very helpful in difficult times.

> *What others think of you is none of your business*
> *What you think of them is none of their business*

Pass this message onto your child. Really show him how true these words are. What other people think of your child is their own thoughts, not your child's own thoughts, and they are of no business for your child to listen to. The same is true the other way around, what your child thinks of others is of no business to those others. Once I got this message, I could see more clearly that we all are allowed to have our own opinions but that we are not allowed to take in others opinions that don't ring true for us and that we are not allowed to force our opinions on others. This may be a very empowering message for your child to understand.

How often does your child feel depressed, angry, frustrated, and/or defensive? Are you at a loss for why your child's life is the way it is? Do you find that your child lashes out at others because of his own frustrations? We often lash out as a defensive mechanism. We may do this because we feel powerless, and victimized. Victimhood is not a good thing. It actually disempowers you.

Being a victim will only prolong your child's suffering. What is happening to your child on the outside is actually a reflection of what is happening to him on the inside. Help your child to understand that he is NOT a victim. That the things that happen to him may be because of his own beliefs about himself and that there is always a lesson that can be learned from everything that we experience. Let him know that there are no mistakes, but only opportunities to learn. If he changes how he thinks about himself then he will change how the world around him will mirror his inner thoughts. Don't ever let him forget that he matters! He doesn't deserve this way of life, he really doesn't. He must come to realize that at an inner level that he deserves the absolute best in life so that he can reflect that out to the Universe to get it back in return.

Open up a way to communicate with your child. Offer him a safe place to open up and share his feeling and thoughts. Be positive and supportive without criticism. Give him a chance to ask anything he needs to know. Be honest and appropriate for his age. Don't worry. There is hope. There IS a solution.

Make the time to sit down with your child and watch the classic movie, "It's a wonderful life". In the movie there comes a point when George Bailey, the main character, reaches his absolute deepest grief of hopelessness and desperation and declares, "The world would be better off if I never lived." However like in the movie, we don't realize how many people we touch every day in our lives. Some small thing we do today might save someone's life tomorrow. You don't have to believe in fate to know we all affect one another. Please make the time to sit down and watch this movie with your child, especially if he is reaching a critical point in his life. It just may open up his eyes to the fact that there is a way out; that the world would NOT be better off if he had never lived.

Just a simple smile or kind word to another can pass on a most positive effect that your child may never even realize he has caused.

We are surrounded with help. We have tools all around us, in people, movies, music, books. Take advantage of these, use them. Get your child signed up with your local library and make a point of going there and getting him the inspiration and motivation he needs. These tools can help your child to become truly self-aware. Aware of how much control he really does have in his own life.

Hope is our way out; it's your child's way out. Knowing he deserves to find the way out is his first step. Knowing where to find the way out is his next step, you can help him with that by providing him the tools that he needs. The fact that you are reading this book shows you that you are moving forward, you are truly seeking the help your child needs. So, keep reading and be open to creating positive results in your child's life, and in your own life as well.

Intention is powerful. You have to get crystal clear on your exact intention here to achieve the results that you want for your child. Like in the book, "The 7 Habits of Highly Effective People," you have to "begin with the end in mind." Knowing where you want your child to end up is essential, and knowing where he IS now is the first step to planning your path along the road to helping your child to get there.

If you believe it's possible, you can help your child believe it too, and find his way there.

Story:
Scotty Learns About "THE PERFECT DAY"

"You'll never amount to anything. You're a LOSER!" Brett yelled at Scottie.

Scottie felt the blood drain into his toes. He felt hollow inside because he knew that Brett was right, he WAS a loser. Everyone knew that. He couldn't even tie his own shoes without tying them together.

"Hey what's up Scottie?" Suzy asked as she sat down next to him on the cement step outside their school entrance, waiting for their school bus to arrive.

"Nothing," Scottie replied.

"Come on, you can tell me," Suzy encouraged.

Suzy was Scottie's "super happy" next-door neighbor. It drove Scottie crazy that Suzy always seemed to have everything she ever wanted. When they were five, Suzy said she wanted a bike, and then two days later Scottie saw her riding her new bike down their street.

Another time Suzy said she was going to a wax museum. There was no was museum anywhere nearby, and there was no way that Suzy could have gone into one of the closest cities to go and see one. So he asked her, "How do you know you're going to a wax museum? There are no wax museums here."

"I know I will, because I decided I will, and I know exactly what it will be like when I'm there."

"So why bother going if you already know what it feels like?"

"You're right, why bother?" Suzy replied mischievously.

Suzy looked at Scottie's perplexed facial expression and continued with, "You know what Scottie? One day you're going to ask me about the 'Perfect Day'."

"Huh?" Scottie replied but Suzy had already run off to get on their bus.

"So what's the 'Perfect Day', Suzy?" Scottie continued their conversation as he caught up with her and joined the line-up to get on their bus.

"Hold on I'll explain in a minute" She said.

They both moved towards the bus door. They wanted to get a seat in the back of the bus before the bullies did.

As they entered the bus, they could hear snickers and a low whisper, "Look here comes the LOSER!"

Suzy ignored them completely, didn't even seem to notice them. She sat down in the back left seat and patted the seat next to her. Scottie took the offered seat and tried to ignore the comments coming from the front of the bus but he could never completely drown them out.

"How do you do that?" he asked her. "Do what?" she replied.

"How can you ignore those jerks?" Scottie pointed to the front of the bus.

"Oh them, they don't have anything that I need to hear, so I don't even hear them at all. What did they say?" she asked Scottie.

"They call me a LOSER".

"Do you believe them?" Suzy looked right at Scottie with pure curiosity in her eyes.

"I guess so, I mean I always flunk the tests, and I can't even tie my own shoes without tying them together." He answered.

"Then you're right!" she stated.

He just sat there absolutely shocked. He thought she was his friend and now here she was telling him that he was a loser.

"Thanks a lot Suzy!"

"Hey, you said it. If you say it's true, then it is. Remember my 'perfect day'?" she asked.

"Hey, don't change the subject; I want to know why you think I'm a loser." Scottie was feeling the heat rise to his cheeks.

"I didn't say it, you did. And, I'm not changing the subject, so do you remember my 'perfect day'?" she replied with absolute calmness.

"Yeah, sure, your 'perfect day'" Scottie replied a little less enthusiastically. "Do you remember the time I wanted to go to that wax museum?"

"I sure do, I was mystified. How did you do it? There are no museums here at all, and your parents couldn't take you all the way to the big city and yet, you went with that crazy lady I saw come to your house. I don't even know who she was or how you managed to get her to take you all the way to the city to see the wax museum. The photo she took of you with Arnold Schwarzenegger looked so real and boy did you look tiny next to him!" Scottie smiled remembering the day she showed him the photo.

"That's the one" she giggled. "Well, I didn't know that my Aunt Maud would be coming for a visit or that she would ask my parents if she could take me for a fun day to the city. I was just as surprised as you were. But I wasn't surprised, when we walked along the sidewalk in the city and we walked right past a wax museum. Even before I could turn around and go back and beg and plead with my Aunt to take me there, a guy in the street handed my Aunt a flyer with a 50% off the admission price for that wax museum.

Well, my Aunt just turned to me and asked, 'what do you think? Shall we have a look inside?' I was flabbergasted, it had happened just as I had written in my 'perfect day'"

"So what's a 'perfect day'?" Scottie was now dying with curiosity.

"Your 'Perfect Day' is an exact description of how you would like to live your absolutely perfect day. You write about everything that will happen to you on this perfect day. You don't leave out ANY details. Even things like what you will eat for your meals. I wrote that I would eat a huge Weiner dog with sauerkraut, and that is definitely not something we would get to eat at home but when I went to the big city with my Aunt, we walked right up to one of those street vendors and that is EXACTLY what I ate!"

"Wow!"

"You should give it a try." Suzy encouraged. "Me?"

"Sure," Suzy pushed him on the shoulder, "especially you." She smiled. "You need to write it out more than anyone else I know."

"I don't think it will work for me" Scottie hung his head. "Well not with THAT attitude!" Suzy exclaimed.

"Huh?"

"Do you know that you are the reason that you have such awful days?" said Suzy. "What?" said Scottie?

"Yup! If you would just BELIEVE that you would have GREAT days, then you WOULD! It's really that simple." She said.

"You mean I have awful days and people are mean to me because that's what I'm asking for? What I want to happen? This is ridiculous. I don't want to be called a LOSER!" Scottie said in disbelief.

"But you do. Don't you see, you think you're a loser, so you naturally attract people to you that confirm your own thoughts. You asked me before why I can ignore those guys. Well, I honestly don't even hear them. Truly. I do hear all the nice things that I want to hear though. And I experience all the nice things I want to experience. I didn't always you know." Suzy stated.

"Really?" Scottie was intrigued.

"Of course not! There are very few people who know about the 'perfect day' secret naturally. We all have to learn it; we have to experience it to finally believe that it truly works. And it does." Suzy took a breath. "Do you remember that bike I got? You were so impressed that I got it after I had asked for it just a few days before. Remember?"

"I could never figure that out." Scottie nodded.

"Well, you see the day before I asked, I saw a guy on TV talking about 'the perfect day' so I wanted to try it out to see if it really could happen for me. Can you remember the difference in my tone when I told you I was going to get a new bike and the time I told you I was going to a wax museum?"

"Sure, you were super confident about the wax museum, I even believed you would achieve that after I saw what happened with the bike thing." Scottie coaxed.

"That's right. I was super confident it would work because I had seen it work for my bike. Did I ever tell you how I got my bike Scottie?"

"No, I never figured that one out."

"Well, after watching the guy on the TV, I went straight to my bedroom and grabbed my colored pencil crayons and a piece of paper from my mom's printer. I sat at my desk and drew the exact bike that I wanted. I colored it in with the colors I wanted."

"Yeah, it was all rainbows!" Scottie interrupted.

"Right. Then I did what the guy on TV said to do. I wrote out my perfect day, what I would eat, what I would play and I especially put in the words, 'I am so happy and grateful now that I am riding my brand new rainbow bike.' I nearly fell over when a guy walked up the street the day I got that bike to ask my dad if he could give me his little girls old bike. He even apologized because his daughter had painted it all sorts of crazy colors but was insistent that it was in good shape. She had outgrown it and he didn't know anyone else with a little girl and thought I might like to have it. I couldn't believe my ears. He didn't even want any money for it. My dad didn't want to just take it for nothing, so he gave the man some of Mom's ripe tomatoes as a way of saying thanks."

"So that's how you got it." Scottie was starting to understand.

"You know the funny thing?" Suzy asked him.

"What?" Scottie questioned.

"I had also written that there would be lots of ripe tomatoes that day! It was my first year that I was allowed to help mom with her garden and I remember working so hard weeding around and watering the tomatoes."

"That's so cool." Scottie was amazed. "So you think I can do this too?" "If you think you can than you can," was Suzy's reply.

"You keep saying that."

"What?" Suzy asked.

"If I think I can then I can, if I think I am then I am." Scottie said.

"Well it's true. I thought I could have a new bike and I did. I thought I could go inside a wax museum and I did. Both times I had the odds against me. I had no clue HOW these things would happen I just knew they would, and they did!" Suzy's enthusiasm was starting to rub off on Scottie.

"Okay, I'll do it!" he said.

"Great! I'll help you if you want." Suzy offered.

"Oh would you? That would be great!" Scottie beamed.

"Sure, hey what friends are for?" and she gathered her bag as the bus slowed to their stop.

As they got off the bus, Suzy yelled, "I'll be over in about ten minutes, just need to say hi to mom. Get your paper ready and see if you can find some old magazines. See you soon."

"Thanks Suzy!" Scottie yelled after her.

Activity 1

Questions from the story:

- Why do you think the other boys constantly bully Scottie?
- Why would they bully Scottie but not Suzy?
- What was the magic formula for Suzy?
- What was the key reason her magic formula worked?
- If Scottie tried "the perfect day" in his own life, do you think it will help him?
- Would it do any harm?

Useful questions to ask your child and write down together:

- What do I want more of in my life?
- How do I affect others, both positively and negatively? How do I want my life to change?
- What are some small ways I can make a change?

Activity 2

Materials: old magazines, paper, colored pencils, pen, scissors, glue

- Have your children write out what they would like to change in their life, what would their perfect day look like for them?
- What would they do when they woke up? What would they eat for breakfast?
- Who would they eat it with?
- What would they do in the morning? Who would they do it with?
- What would they eat for lunch? Who would they eat it with?
- What would they do in the afternoon? Who would they play with?
- What would they play? Where would they go?
- How long would they go for? What are their friends like?
- How do their friends inspire and motivate them? What kind of books would they read?
- What kind of movies would they watch? What kind of things would they study? What would they eat for dinner?
- Who would they eat it with?
- What would they do in the evening? Where would they go?
- Who would they do it with?
- What would they think about before going to bed at night?
- Most importantly, have them write how would they feel as it was all happening?

After they write out their perfect day, have them go through the old magazines (or search for photos on the internet and print them out) and cut out photos that represent their perfect day. Then cut out the individual sections of their written perfect day. Then have them paste them in order on a new sheet. So they would paste first a written section then paste a corresponding photo(s). Then the next section and next photo(s), etc. until they have their entire perfect day put onto paper with both hand written text and corresponding photos. Now hang up their perfect day papers (and there may be many) on the walls in their bedroom so they can see their perfect day on a very regular basis.

Note (the magic ingredient): Make sure when writing down their perfect day they use PRESENT tense (i.e. "I am eating a waffle with whipped cream and a huge ripe, sweet strawberry on top", Not "I will be eating...") Writing their perfect day as if they are living it in this very moment is key to this working.

Activity 3

Think back to your own life and share a story that relates to this topic, and discuss how you felt at their age, and what you learned from it.

2 There is a Way Out for Your Child

*"You can't solve a problem with
the same mind that created it."*
Albert Einstein

There is a way out for your child, really! No matter what, your child will always have a way out! Sometimes you or your child will keep on trying to solve the same problem with the same thinking, and then come to believe that there truly is no way out. But there is! Sometimes when your child is right in the middle of an "upset," she will really think that she is accurately aware of her own feelings and of how she is thinking in that moment.

However, the problem remains that she is "upset." To be "upset" by definition, means that you aren't centered in your feelings, and more importantly, you often aren't centered in your thinking. There may be many reasons why your child will be upset, and we can't address all of them here. What you can do for your child when she is upset, is to help her make better decisions, and to think more clearly. I've written another short story at the end of this chapter for you to read together with your child to help demonstrate the way that she can make better decisions and think more clearly in her moments of "upset."

Sometimes she will need to blow off steam, which is fine, as long as she is able to do so without hurting anyone else or herself in the process.

The optimum person to help your child with this would be a neutral witness. You will often not be the neutral witness that she needs. Please don't take it personally. It's not about you. It's about her. It may seem as if a neutral witness would be hard to come by but your child actually has her very own neutral witness inside of her. You can help her to become aware of her own neutral witness. You can remind her in her moments of 'upset' to look within herself, and find that special neutral part of her.

The challenge is going to be for her to find this part of herself. Her ego will most likely be blocking her from doing this. We all have a part of us that does the main thinking, and that is our ego. Sometimes we just need to step back from our ego and let our intuition and our neutral witness come through.

To access your inner neutral witness, you need to get quiet and be still so you can "hear" your subconscious mind. There will be different thoughts that come to your mind, but don't fight them. That is your ego. Anytime you feel your own ego getting in your way, just simply pause, and then give it thanks for protecting you and ask it to please move aside to let your intuition and your neutral witness come through. By giving your ego thanks for the wonderful protection that it is doing for you, you are making it feel appreciated and it won't be so adept at wanting to constantly get your attention.

By feeling these different parts of yourself, you are better able to recognize and help your own child recognize the different parts of herself. Once you are able to ask your ego to step aside for a moment of clarity then you will be able to access this unbiased witness, the part of you that knows the answer.

Then you can help your child do the same for herself. The old expression was, "Take a deep breath and count to 10, and then see what answer comes to you." I encourage you to tell your child to take 3 slow deep breaths and then see how they feel. Chances are they will be more balanced, and make a better decision.

Here's an exercise you can do with your child to help her find that inner neutral witness:

First, ask her to stop what she is doing and separate herself from what's causing her upset. Ask her to take three deep breaths. Okay, now have her clear her mind for a minute. Just concentrate on her breathing. Concentrate on what's going on inside of herself. Just relax and breathe. If she believes in a higher power, have her ask for calming clarity. Have her take a few minutes to center herself. This may be all it takes for her to be able to approach her upset and resolve the problem.

Sometimes you'll have to have her release even more of the energy surrounding her upset. Most often, when she can slow down for a moment, she will be able to adjust herself to a more centered position. When she is very off-center, she might need more than a moment. (We will cover more on how to release emotional energy in Chapter 9.) Once that release is accomplished, she may or may not be back at center. Sometimes it takes more than one process of releasing before she will feel balanced, and sometimes once will do it. It all depends on how upset she was to begin with. If she finds that her ego keeps on getting in the way, then have her add the exercise of thanking her ego for the protection it gives her and that she appreciates very much ego's important role, and then ask ego to step aside for a moment so she can reach her inner neutral witness. If she is still out of balance after all of that, don't have her try to make any important decisions. Just have her relax and know that it will get better. That it's probably not as bad as it may seem. There are many other methods. Choose which one works best for your child.

The important thing for to her to realize is, everything happening to her is for her highest good; although it often doesn't seem so at the time.

There is always something for her to learn from each interaction in her life. The question to have her ask herself is, "What can I learn from this?" Her ego will have one response, but her heart will have the answer that will benefit her highest good. Just have her look and see which is which. Always have her choose what is for her highest good. Sometimes she won't see the answer right away. You can feel free to show her some options, just make sure that you bring it across to her as options, not definite answers, she needs to come up with her own answers. It can be tricky to handle your child in this way, but with each practice you will learn and your bond with her will seem more natural. Over time she will get less defensive as she sees her own way out of her problems. Just remember to be her constant cheerleader, no matter what. That is what she needs most, to know that you believe that she can make her own right decisions. And she will.

Remember: Just because she can't see a way out, it doesn't mean there isn't one, two, or more! Why not help her believe that she has a way out? She has everything to gain!

"We shall never cease from exploration
And the end of all our exploring
Will be to arrive where we started
And know the place for the first time."
– T.S. Eliot

Story: James Finds His Inner Voice

James stopped to catch his breath. He'd been running for what seemed like hours in circles. He knew he just had to find the river, cross it and he would finally be able to get the help his dad so urgently needed. It would be dark soon and then he wouldn't be able to find his way through the forest. He couldn't camp the night either, his dad needed him to find help right away. James was a city boy and he was terrified of the dark forest.

His dad had been driving them back home after a fun week of Spring break holidays. Then he hit a stone on the road that blew his tire, and had sent them careening into the forest. The car had buckled and his dad had been trapped against the steering wheel. His dad was thoroughly pinned in and there was no way that he could get out on his own.

"Dad, you're bleeding" James was horrified. "You're going to have to get help son."

"Where? We're in the forest, there's no gas station anywhere and we haven't passed another car in hours. What if no one comes, Dad? What are we going to do?" James could feel the hopelessness building inside him. He couldn't help his dad out of the car. The gouge on his dad's leg was huge, and he couldn't get to it to tie off the bleeding. He really felt helpless and so scared.

"I'll be fine son. You need to find help. Here have a look at the map." His dad motioned to the glove box. James opened the box and took out the map. They had a look and there was a Bed & Breakfast nearby. It would be about 20 miles by road, since the road had to go around the lake first to get there. They could see that it was only about 3 miles away if James took a short cut through the forest. He'd have to cross a river, but there was a walking bridge, and he'd be able to get the help his dad so desperately needed faster. There was no real choice. He had to take the short cut.

James looked up at his dad with a worried look in his eyes.

"It's okay James, really. I'll be okay, but I need you to go there now and get help right away. I can't get to my leg to stop the bleeding and I won't have too much time before I faint. When you come back I'll probably have already fainted. So please do not worry, I have no intention of leaving you." he gave James a weak smile, "I know you can do this James. I trust in you. Trust in yourself. Now go." He said firmly.

James reached over and kissed his dad on his cheek, "I love you Dad". "I love you too James. Go now."

James grabbed the map and opened the door. He slammed it shut and ran into the forest. He knew he had to follow the setting sun to get to the Bed & Breakfast, it would lead him there.

He'd been running about ten minutes through the woods, following the path of the sun and was sure he was on the right track when he'd heard a rustling in trees to his left. Panic immediately set in, and he jumped ahead and ran with all his might for what seemed like hours; desperately trying to stay in line of the sun.

Finally he had to stop and catch his breath. Maybe it wasn't a bear, maybe it was just a bird or a squirrel he had heard but he didn't want to take his chances. He knew that there were both black bears and coyotes here in the forest and he needed to get help for his dad, quick! He was so worried. "I WILL save my Dad!" he declared out loud.

Just then he heard the rushing of water. His spirits lifted and he ran in the direction of the sound. Within a minute he was standing at the edge of the river. It was getting dark and the trail was hard to see to find the walking bridge.

He started to panic with the sun going down. The map said it should be close by, so he kept walking. He spluttered to catch his breath and then tried to fight the fear and find the bridge to get to the other side, but it was no use. The forest just kept on getting darker. The currents in the middle were too strong for him to cross. He finally gave up in despair and sat down on a large boulder.

Finally he let his tears of grief and anger come. How could he fail his dad? Why wasn't he strong enough to fight the river, or to find the bridge to cross to the other side? He could even see the lights of the Bed & Breakfast now peeping through the trees. He stood up and screamed at the top of his lungs for help.

"Please someone hear me. Help. My dad needs help!" he yelled, but to no use. He was still too far away for anyone to hear him and the rushing of the river just drowned out his yells. His voice was raw and sore. He felt useless. His Dad was going to die and he was going to be eaten alive by bears and coyotes. He just knew it!

His mom and sister would hate him. They would blame him for not saving his dad. It was all his fault! He sat down again and sobbed out from his soul. He didn't know what else to do.

In the silence that he found within his cries, he heard a voice. "Listen to me" it said.

James stopped crying immediately and turned around to see who was there. No one was there.

It was getting really dark now. And his dad…

"Ohhh…." He cried. The moan coming from deep within him.

"I'm here for you, if you'll listen to me." The voice said.

James stopped his crying and closed his eyes to listen. He didn't know who or what was talking to him, but he was all cried out and he had nowhere to go. So he just took a deep breath in and listened.

From deep inside himself he could hear the little voice becoming clearer, "You need to take yourself out of this problem."

"What? How can I do that? This IS my problem, my dad's going to die, and it's all my fault!" James screamed out at the voice.

"Is your problem bigger than you or are you bigger than your problem," came the reply. "Huh?" James was uncertain of the meaning.

"Whichever is bigger will take control." The voice persisted. "I'm bigger." James said.

"Are you?" the voice inside questioned.

"Yes!" James was determined to take control. He could solve this.

"Okay, then go outside yourself. What do you see?" the voice continued.

"I see me sitting here on the rock by the river that I can't cross." James immediately felt hopeless again. "Snap out of it!" the voice shouted inside of James.

"Huh?" James came out of his grief and guilt once more. "Look further, what else do you see?" it questioned James.

"I see huge trees, they are very tall. I see boulders. I see the river and the lights of the Bed & Breakfast on the other side."

"Okay, what can you use with what you see to find a solution?" "I don't know…" James was confused.

"Take a deep breath" James did. "Okay, now look again what do you see? How do the trees and boulders look to you?" the voice insisted.

"Okay, I see the huge trees. Their branches are low. The boulders are smooth and round. "Which one would be useful to you right now?"

"I don't understand." James was so confused and so worried about his dad.

"Let him go for now, James. He will be alright as long as you let him go right now and open yourself up for the solution to come through to you."

"I know!" James stood up. "The trees!" he stated.

James ran to the nearest, tallest, strongest tree he could get to. He climbed up the tree as high as he could.

"Look" the voice inside said.

"I can see the Bed & Breakfast" James said. "Look further" The voice replied.

"Oh I see it!" James scampered down the tree and ran down along the river. He hadn't been able to see it before because he had been blinded by his own grief, guilt, anger, and helplessness. About 200 yards away was the foot bridge across the river. He ran with all his might. He'd found the way!

His dad would be safe. He knew it!

Activity 1

Questions from the story

- What was blocking James' vision of the bridge? How did James blow off his steam?
- What did he have to do to be able to listen to his inner neutral witness? What happened to James when he finally listened to his inner voice?
- How did it make him feel?
- Useful questions to ask your child and write down together
- No matter how seemingly impossible, what are some of my ways out?
- How have I blown off steam? Are there any other, better ways to blow off steam? What is the bigger picture?
- What are the tools I can use in my life that can help me overcome the problem, or at least to deal with the problem?
- What can I learn from the problem that will help me to grow and be better prepared for life's next lesson for me?

Activity 2

Take a piece of paper and draw the following chart and fill it in together with your child to come up with some solutions for any future problems that may or are likely to come her way. (Add more pages as you need them.)

Problem	How would it make you feel?	What tools can you use to help you?	Who can help you?	What are some solutions	How will it feel to solve your problem?
1.					
2.					
3.					
4.					

Activity 3

Think back to your own life and share a story that relates to this topic, and discuss how you felt at their age, and what you learned from it.

Autobiography in Five Short Chapters by Portia Nelson

1. I walk down the street
   There is a deep hole in the sidewalk.
   I fall in, I am lost… I am helpless.
   It isn't my fault.
   It takes me forever to find my way out.

2. I walk down the same street.
   There is a deep hole in the sidewalk.
   I pretend I don't see it, I fall in again.
   I can't believe I'm in the same place. But it isn't my fault.
   It still takes me a long time to get out.

3. I walk down the same street.
   There is a deep hole in the sidewalk.
   I see it there, I still fall in… It's a habit.
   My eyes are open.
   I know where I am.
   It is my fault.
   I get out immediately.

4. I walk down the same street.
   There is a deep hole in the sidewalk.
   I walk around it.

5. I walk down another street.

"Whether you think you can or that you can't, you're right."
– Henry Ford

John Seeley M.A. & Amanda van der Gulik

3   Miracles Happen Every Day

"Miracles are like jokes. They relieve our tension suddenly by setting us free from the chain of cause and effect."
– Gerald Branan

Whether you believe in the law of gravity or not, it exists. The same goes for whether you believe in the law of miracles or not, miracles do happen. We are powerful creators. There is a power to create anything and it resides in our imaginative mind. Your child can create his own miracles. The key is that he has to believe, or at least be open to a miracle happening.

Miracles come in all sizes. Your child may not even recognize that what is happening is a miracle. It might look like a close call, or it could be a traffic jam that delays him from being involved in an accident. It might be a call from someone he was thinking about. It could be the loss of a grade – that points out what is NOT his life passion, a subject not necessarily meant for him to follow – allowing your child to change subjects to something that makes his heart sing. It could be a chance meeting where he ends up forming a lifelong relationship. It could be that bike that he wanted is finally on sale, right when he has earned the money to buy it.

The question to have him ask himself is, "What miracle do you want to happen?"

Let him imagine that he has a magic wand and he can have ANYTHING he wants. What would it be? Have him use his imagination. There is no boundary to his wants and desires. What does he really want? Let him know that it is OKAY for him to ask for ANYTHING. Ask him, "What would you ask for if you knew for absolute certain that you would get it?" Now have him give this a try. Have him pick something he wants. Have him get a crystal clear picture of it in his mind. How does it look? What color is it? How does it feel? Does it have a smell or a taste? Have him focus on it until he can practically have it in his hand.

Then have him think of this feeling every single day, in the morning when he wakes up, and at night when he goes to bed. Have him visualize it with all of his senses. Have him open his eyes to where this wish may show up. It may show up on an ad on TV or it may appear just outside his window. It could show up at school; anywhere! Someone might bring up the same object or situation to him in a conversation. Have him watch and see where it shows up. It will. It's a miracle.

Miracles are often created by our intentions. It may take a little time. You son will need to really pay attention to his intentions. If he has two opposing intentions then they will cancel each other out or just come out all mixed up. If he pays attention to the results he will begin to notice when his intentions are bumping into each other. Whichever result he has will be because of the strongest intention, and this will be a good way for him to gauge his intentions and their strength.

You may hear him saying something like, "I wish I could afford a brand new iPod, but I don't have enough money." In this case even though he is wishing for the new iPod, his "but I don't have enough money" is winning. It is the stronger intention. He will never have enough money because that is what he is unconsciously intending. This is a good time to go over any of his underlying beliefs that have been keeping him from getting what he really wants. Have him take the time to really focus on the things he wants and get him to write them down.

There is a magic in actually writing down your goals, wants and desires. It's almost like writing a contract, or a 'Santa Wish List', you will most likely get what you write down. Have him try it, he'll be pleasantly surprised. But make sure he writes only positive words, "I will have...", "I am grateful for...", "I appreciate it now that I..." and make sure he writes in the present tense: "I have," NOT "I will have." There is a huge difference to the outcomes these small changes make.

Have him make different categories. What does he want to be when he grows up? What kind of job or profession or business would he like to have? What would he like in his personal life, in his relationships with his friends, his family, his future partner? How much money would he like to earn every month?

What is his ideal health like? What kinds of things would he like to do? Where would he like to visit? Would he like to grow spiritually? In what way?

Have him make a list for each individual area of his life. Now, add to his list why he 'thinks' he can't or hasn't been able to get these results. Have him look at his list of obstacles. Are they really preventing him? Is fear or something in particular holding him back? Is he letting his fear create his intentions? He can choose his own beliefs. Think about that. It's true. Why not encourage him to choose what he really wants? Help him to let the miracles begin!

> *"There are only two ways to live your life.
> One is as though nothing is a miracle.
> The other is as though everything is a miracle."*
> *- Albert Einstein*

Story: Not Such a PERFECT DAY for Scottie

"Hey Scottie, how're things going with your 'Perfect Day'?" Suzy asked as she sat down next to him at lunch the next day. Suzy had gone over to Scottie's house after dropping her bag off at home and letting her mom know where she would be. Scottie's mom had even invited her to stay for the yummy pizza she had made for them. This had given Suzy the time she needed to help Scottie go over his goals and dreams of how his 'Perfect Day' would go.

"Not that great," Scottie replied moodily. "Brent pushed me down this morning and I flunked the geography test in class today."

"Well, you need to give the universe time to make things happen." Suzy encouraged.

"You never give up do you Suzy?"

"Nope!" she smiled at him, "Besides if I did then I wouldn't be living the life I want to live. I intend to win in life. Life is easy, life is good, life is rewarding. Those are my chosen thoughts and that is how I now really see life. You want to know a secret to making your 'perfect day' come faster?"

"Boy, do I ever! Anything to get Brent to leave me alone would be great!" Scottie was feeling really down on himself this morning. He had spent hours creating his 'perfect day' yesterday and he had fully expected that he would see a change today already. And nothing! He'd even flunked the test. He was sure this was never going to work.

"Hey, don't be so hard on yourself," Suzy continued. "Okay, the secret ingredient is that you need to go back to your list of wants, goals and desires and write down every excuse in the world that you can think up as to WHY you WON'T get your wishes."

"What? That would be WAY TOO depressing!" Scottie sure didn't want to do that! He had had so much fun writing down his goals and dreams and he couldn't believe that she was asking him to now go back and make each single one negative by writing down all the reasons that he wouldn't be able to achieve his goals. It sounded like hard, depressing work.

"I know it sounds like a really awful way to go over your list but you'll see it will start to open you up to your true inside feelings of WHY you have not been getting what you want in life. It will not actually stop you from getting your goals. It will actually help you to better understand what it is deep down inside of you that has been stopping you from getting what you want. Get it?" Suzy asked.

"I guess so, but I sure don't want to do it. It was so much fun writing down what I WOULD be getting and I don't want to kill that feeling." Scottie said.

"Don't you see? Look at yourself. You're sitting slumped over, your eyes are down, your face has a frown, your whole body is screaming out, 'I never get what I want!' So you can't possibly be still feeling great about the job we did last night or you would be sitting very differently."

Suzy had a point. Scottie could see that. "Okay, I guess you're right. But won't I be attracting the things I don't want by writing down my reason why I CAN'T get my dreams?"

"That's a very good question Scottie, and I completely understand your concern. You have finally let yourself open up to the possibility of creating the future you want for yourself and you don't want to lose that right?" Suzy asked.

"Yeah, that's exactly how I feel, how did you know?" Scottie questioned. "Don't you think that happens to me sometimes too?"

"Oh, I hadn't thought about that, you just seem to always get what you want. I didn't know you ever doubted that."

"Are you kidding? Do you think I'm super human or something? Get real." Suzy said with disbelief. "I get down too, you know. Everyone does. I just choose not to let my down moments rule my life. That's the difference. I've found that whenever I feel like giving up on a goal that seems just too crazy for me to ever get, the ONLY way I can get my head around it is to go deep inside and figure out why I feel I can't have that wish.

"It must be to do with how I feel inside about myself, because the Universe doesn't care what I feel. It only cares what messages I am sending out. So if I've asked for something and done it in the right, positive, present tense way and it still doesn't happen, then it's usually because somewhere deep down inside I'm sending contradicting messages to the Universe. Does this make sense Scottie?"

"I guess so. So let's say that when you wanted that cool bike deep down inside you were actually afraid to ride it. Your subconscious would be sending out another message that said something like, 'I can't ride that bike' so your message that you were sending out at a stronger feeling was that you should never get the bike because you couldn't ride it anyway. Is that what you mean Suzy?" Scottie was starting to figure it out and was starting to feel more inspired by this new idea of getting to the bottom of the feelings each goal generated in him.

"You've got it!" Suzy smiled proudly. The bell rung to end the lunch break. "Hey, I'll come over again tonight after dinner and we can start to go over your goals and figure out what is stopping them from coming to you. Okay?"

"That would be great. Thanks Suzy, you're great!" Scottie felt excited again and couldn't wait for his classes to end.

"Hey, one more thing?" Suzy yelled back at him over her shoulder just before she got to the cafeteria door.

"What?"

"This is only the beginning. After we get to the bottom of your inner fears, then we'll send out a new even more powerful message to the Universe to help you get what you want." Suzy smiled.

"How?" Scottie wanted to know.

"I'll tell you about it tonight. Expect the best!" she reminded him as she ran to get her books for class.

Activity 1

Questions from the story

Why was Scottie feeling so low about himself at lunch?

What was it that Suzy said he needed to do now with his 'Perfect Day' dream list?

Why did Scottie need to look at his feelings about each of his dreams?

How did Scottie feel after talking to Suzy?

What had made him feel this way?

What did Suzy yell out to Scottie when she left?

What did it mean?

Useful questions to ask your child and write down together

What miracles have shown up in your life?

What intentions are you telling the world? (If you don't know, look at your results)

What do you really want that you don't have?

What miracles would you like to have in your life?

Activity 2:

Go back to your Chapter 1 Activity, and get out your child's 'Perfect Day' project.

Use the following chart to write out each individual goal and help your child to find out what inner blocks they may have had for each goal. Add more pages as you need them.

	"Perfect Day" Dream/Goal	Why You Believe You *Won't* Get Your Goals
Wish		
Wish		
Wish		
Wish		
Wish		

Activity 3

Think back to your own life and share a story that relates to this topic, and discuss how you felt at their age, and what you learned from it.

"Where there's a will, there's a way."
– Proverb

John Seeley M.A. & Amanda van der Gulik

4   Growth vs. Decay

"All growth is a leap in the dark, a spontaneous unpremeditated act without benefit of experience."
– Henry Miller

According to Socrates, there are three phases to how humans progress through life: first we grow through a period of growth, then we plateau, and finally we decay. Later Plato came along and said we grow and decay. That's it. Basically, if you look at a tree, it's growing until someone cuts it down. Then it begins to decay. You can make a table from it – which seems like a plateau – but it's actually slowly decaying, slowly, but decaying.

We as humans are perpetually growing and decaying. Our cells re-grow regularly, so that you literally are not the person you used to be. More importantly, when it comes to mentality and emotion, you are either growing or decaying. Your child has a choice. She can either choose to continue to grow, to learn new things or give in and start to decay. It's really up to her. We don't have to decay until the end of our days unless we simply choose to no longer grow.

Your child will learn eighty percent of her "programs" (her unconscious behavior patterns), by the time she is eight-years-old. She will learn another fifteen percent by the time she reaches eighteen-years-old. This leaves her with five percent of her programs for the rest of her life. Therefore, she will have an eight-year-old running her life a lot of the time for the rest of her life, and that might not be the best thing for her. The great news is that she can use the five percent to change the other ninety-five percent. And you can help her to change any negative behaviors while she is young so that she will have better programs to run her. Now is the time to get started, don't make her wait to change unwanted habits later.

Some of the programs that your child will learn in the early years have been key to her growth this far: potty training is a good example of this. Walking is another. She will create programs that work for her as a child but will not work for her as an adult. For example she may find that hiding in her room as a child helps her to hide from someone or something, but as she grows up she will need to learn that she must face her fears head on.

Facing her fears will quite often be the last thing that she will want to do but avoiding them won't make them disappear. You can help her to recognize these emotions while she is still young so that she will be better able to face them head on when she is older. Having her admit she is afraid will be her first step to getting past her fear. Once she admits what she is afraid of she will begin to form a new plan for dealing with her fears.

She will need to get support in dealing with her fears. Support can come from you and your own experiences that you can share with her. It may come from a book about how someone else faced his or her fear. It could be from a friend who listens to her and encourages her to move forward without any bias that you may have as her parent. You need to find the best support for your child, which may sometimes not be what you were hoping for. We, as parents, often times want to FIX everything for our child ourselves, but sometimes we just need to let go and accept help from others. You may even want to approach a coach or a therapist where your child can verbalize her fears and get advice on how to best deal with her challenges. Once your child chooses to deal with her fears instead of hiding from them, she will begin growing again.

She may simply stop growing because she has stopped being motivated, or has lost hope. If you find your child gets to this place, really encourage her to reach out for help. We all need help once in a while. It may help to show her how you have needed your own help in your own past. She may just need to see that you are normal and that what she feels is normal. Above all, let her know that she can always ask for help, don't let her become afraid to ask for it. Our nature is to seek balance. Even though we may get out of balance and stop growing, it's only temporary. The good thing is your child can always begin to grow again.

"True balance requires assigning realistic performance expectations to each of our roles.
True balance requires us to acknowledge that our performance in some areas
is more important than in others.
True balance demands that we determine what accomplishments give us honest satisfaction as well as what failures cause us intolerable grief."
– Melinda M. Marshall

Story: Lucy Learns a Hard Lesson about Asking For Help

"You must solve this problem on your own," Lucy could hear her teacher's words. Lucy had started to ask Jake to help her with her science project because she'd stumbled upon a problem trying to finish her plant growth graph and she just wasn't 'getting' it. But their teacher, Miss Jones, had seen the request for help and had walked over to them immediately.

"Lucy, you must solve this problem on your own. This is an individual project. We'll work on a team project next week, but I want you to figure this one out on your own please." Miss Jones had said rather sternly.

"I'm sorry Miss Jones, I just don't 'get' this chart. It's not coming together right." Lucy started to explain.

"No, I'm sorry Lucy, but you MUST do this on your own. No help with this one. Sometimes in life you will need to work out problems on your own. So this will be a good experience for you Lucy." With that Miss Jones walked away.

Lucy was at a loss. Her mother had always told her that she could and should always ask for help when she needed it and now her teacher was telling her that she needed to figure out her own answers to her own problems. Lucy figured that Miss Jones must be right, because she was a teacher after all. She was educated and her mother wasn't. Maybe her mother was just trying to help her but didn't really know anything about how to handle life.

It was lunch time and she had not gotten her project done in time and knew she would fail it. But who cares anyway, at least she'd learned that she needed to take care of her own problems and never ask for help. That would serve her well. She was sure. That was more important than her grade she would get on her project.

Lucy could see Sally heading her way and she could instantly feel the hairs on her arms and legs stand on end. Sally was a big-time bully. She usually left Lucy alone but she was headed straight for her and Lucy was dreading the conversation. She just had an instinctive feeling that this was not a social call. Sally was stamping her heavy feet with determination. She looked red in the face. Lucy could clearly see that something had set Sally off.

"Hi Sally" Lucy looked up at her as the girl approached her.

"YOU! It's your fault! You're gonna get it real bad if you don't fix it!" Sally slammed her lunch box down hard on the table, and the force of it tipped over Lucy's water bottle, leaking water all over the table and down onto Lucy's pants leg.

Lucy was at a loss for what to say, she had no idea what Sally was talking about.

"If you don't fix this before end of classes today, I'm going to beat you to a pulp behind the bleachers on the football field after class. You got it?" With that Sally stomped away.

Lucy could feel her heart pump so hard and fast she thought for sure it would break free from her body and run away as fast as it was beating. "What am I going to do?" she asked herself.

Lucy was really scared. She knew that when Sally threatened, she ALWAYS followed through. She felt despair creep inside of her. She couldn't ask for help because Miss Jones had just said this morning that she had to learn to solve problems on her own and she knew this had been what Miss Jones had been talking about. But what on earth could she do? She didn't even know what she had done.

She only had a few minutes left before classes would begin again. She threw her lunch box into her locker and ran to the bathroom. She needed to have a moment to clear her head. She locked herself into a stall and then just leaned against the wall to concentrate, "Okay, think," she thought to herself. "Breathe." A voice inside her head said. She took in a deep breath. "Okay, now what am I going to do?" She asked herself.

Just then she heard the bathroom door open.

"She is SO going to get it after school, the little brat!" Lucy froze to the spot. It was Sally. She didn't dare to breathe. What was she talking about? It didn't really matter. You didn't even need to do anything to get Sally angry with you. She just liked having someone to pick on and beat up. Now it was Lucy's turn. With a building dread, Lucy stayed frozen against the wall in the cubicle as Sally continued her conversation.

"That little idiot tattled to Miss Jones that I cheated on the project this morning. I'm going to get her. I told Miss Jones that it wasn't true, but when she sees the answer I did for section 8, she's going to know I did. Idiot! I hate her, she's really in for it. I'm going to beat her to a pulp!" Sally exclaimed.

Lucy was shocked. She hadn't told on anyone at all and she would never ever consider tattling on Sally. She wasn't stupid! Everyone knew you didn't mess with Sally. Oh what could she do to fix this? Well, she surely couldn't go for help. Miss Jones had just told her that she needed to fix her own problems. This wasn't looking good. Then it came to her, almost as fast and a hard as a bullet. If she could get out of her next class somehow then she could sneak into Miss Jones' office and change Sally's answer to question 8 and then Sally wouldn't be in trouble and she wouldn't want to beat Lucy up anymore.

After Sally left the bathroom, Lucy went off to her next class and found a way to excuse herself. She slipped down into Miss Jones' office and found Sally's project. She was able to change the 8th question and slipped away. Her heart was now pounding so hard she swore that anyone could hear it a mile away. As she slipped back into her seat she caught Sally glaring at her. Now, she'd done it, Sally seemed to be even angrier than before.

"You're in for it!" she mouthed to Lucy, who sank down lower in her chair trying to fade away.

In their last class Miss Jones didn't get Sally into trouble but that just seemed to make Sally even more suspicious.

After class, Sally pushed Lucy in the hall, "Hey idiot, you think you fooled me? I know what you did in class today. You're just trying to save my embarrassment for tomorrow, huh? You hid my project so she would think I didn't do it at all huh? You sure got some nerve kid. I'm getting my stuff, you'd better be at the bleachers in five minutes if you know what's good for you." and with that Sally stormed down the hall to her locker.

What just happened? Lucy was feeling faint. She'd tried to make things better and now they just seemed even worse. How was she supposed to figure this one out on her own? Miss Jones must be wrong, Lucy had to get help, but now it was too late! If she asked for help now, then she'd get into trouble for changing the project. Lucy didn't know what to do. She knew one thing though. She HAD to go to the bleachers or she'd get into even deeper trouble with Sally. Sally ALWAYS kept her promises.

So with that Lucy bravely went to the bleachers. It was awful to say the least. Sally really gave it to her hard. After it was all done and everyone had left Lucy lying there in her own painful world. Lucy's moan could just barely be heard. But Miss Jones heard it. She'd been on her way to her car to go home when she'd heard Lucy's soft moan. She raced over to the bleachers to see what was wrong. She was horrified to see Lucy all curled up in a ball with scratches and bruises all over her face.

"What happened?" she asked.

Lucy's weak reply was, "I solved my problem on my own." "What?" Miss Jones was confused, "What do you mean child?"

"You told me I had to solve my own problems, that when I grew up I would need to work out problems on my own." Lucy cried.

"Oh, Lucy." Miss Jones felt horrible, "I never meant this. What I meant is that you need to reach down deep inside yourself to find your own answers. In this case if you had reached down deep inside yourself you would have learned that you needed to come to me or another teacher for help. We would have never let this happen to you. Are you alright?"

"I'm okay" Lucy mumbled through her bleeding lip.

Miss Jones helped her up onto her feet, "Please promise me Lucy that you will ALWAYS ask for help! I know I must have really confused you today, I'm so sorry, I was wrong to say it to you the way I did. I wish I could take it back. You need to first look deep within you, as to whom to ask for help. Please from now on ask for help when you need it. I was so wrong. I'm sorry Lucy." Miss Jones wrapped Lucy in a firm embrace and took her to the nurse's station to patch her up.

Activity 1

Questions from the story

- What was the message that Miss Jones had given to Lucy without realizing what she had done?
- What would have been a better way for Lucy to handle the misunderstanding with Sally?
- What did Lucy learn in the end?
- What did Miss Jones learn in the end?
- How could Lucy have asked for help in this story?

Useful questions to ask your child and write down together

- What areas in your life are you growing?
- What areas in your life have you been decaying? What areas do you want to make changes in your life?
- How will you be different when you make those changes? Are you willing and ready to ask for help when you need it?

Activity 2

Write out together with your child some of the ways that they can find the help they need.

Personal		
Emotional		
Spiritual		
Academic		
Family		
Bully		
Other		
Other		

Activity 3

Think back to your own life and share a story that relates to this topic, and discuss how you felt at their age, and what you learned from it.

5 Your and Your Child's Word

"A gentleman's word is like a touch of a whip to a racehorse."
– Chinese Proverb

Your child's word is the key to how he feels about himself. How many times has he broken his word? How many times each day have you broken your word yourself? You are your child's role model. He will naturally model that which he experiences through your own actions. If you think that you don't break your own word, then answer some of these questions:

- How many times in the last 24 hours did you say you'd do something and you didn't do it? Did you perhaps promise to return a phone call that you didn't?
- Maybe you promised to be on time for an event and you ended up being late? Maybe you said you'd eat healthy today and you slipped up?
- Or you told yourself you would do a work out and then you didn't find the time for it?
- Possibly you said that you'd obey all the traffic laws, including speeding, and then found yourself slightly over the limit?
- Or that you'd spend some quality time with someone and you didn't?

I could go on and on. Count the times that you broke your word, even if no one even knew about your promises, or caught you breaking your word, one person knows all about them. YOU!

And the same is true for your child. Even if you don't catch him breaking his promises, or his teachers don't, or whoever else, HE still knows, and it is doing damage to his self-esteem. It is also showing himself how much he values himself, if he cannot keep his own promises. He may even end up expecting others not to keep their promises, due to his own feel of lack of self-worth.

Each time he breaks his word, even a little, he is losing some of his own self-esteem. No wonder he doubts his ability to do something, if he's breaking his word daily. Your child's word is the key to how he creates his life. If he doesn't really believe or trust himself, then he won't create what he's really capable of doing. Self-esteem is essential to maximizing your child's potential. Your child may even convince you that he can do a thing, but if he still has an underlying self-doubt, even if it's unconscious, he will have a very tough time completing what he says he wants to do.

Your child's word and how he keeps it, determines how he truly feels about himself.

The good news is that every single time your child keeps his word, his self-esteem goes up and every time you, the parent, keep your word, you are role modeling your own self-worth onto him. So the question then is, "What's your word worth? What's your child's word worth?" Every time you break your word, how do you justify your actions? Have a look and see if you can find the ways in which your child justifies his own actions, each time he breaks his own word. See if he is imitating your own justifications. Think about it for a minute. No matter how good your child is at defending his actions, a part of him will always know that he broke his word. No justification will ever change that. You can't fool yourself, and your child will not be able to fool himself. It's your choice to keep your word or not; and it's your child's own choice to keep his word or not, but you can help him by showing him your own self-worth by keeping your word and then he will automatically begin to role model that into his own life.

Now some people simply don't break their word because they don't commit to anything. This is a program that kids can take on but won't work for them once they are adults. They need to unlearn this as early as they can. This is usually a program that is done unconsciously but you as the parent can spot this when it happens, and encourage him to simply commit to something to break the habit. If you find that your child is not committing to others, chances are he's not committing to himself either. Not committing is self-defeating. If your child won't commit to anything, what can he ever achieve?

Commitment is essential to achievement. Your child might say that he doesn't break his word, but not committing to anything is simply not facing his fears. He doesn't need to be perfect. Non-commitment is trying to be just that, perfect. Being human, by definition, means that we are not perfect. Making commitments and not always keeping them is human. Striving to be the best he can be is all that's required. He doesn't need to be perfect, just to do his best for his own sake, not for the other person's sake. You can help him to realize this by showing him times when you choose commitment over perfection. If you do this enough, he will begin to start role modeling this and begin to raise his self- worth. It's never too late to change. Self-respect and self-esteem are built on your word. Encourage your child to choose what he wants to give his word to. How high would he like his self-esteem to be? How high would you like your own self-esteem to be? You and your child both get to choose.

---

*"Words have the power to both destroy and heal.
When words are both true and kind,
they can change our world."*
– Buddha

Story: Jeannie Doesn't Keep Her Word

"Jeannie, hurry up honey, you're going to be late." mom yelled up the stairs. Jeannie was quickly pulling her hair into the ballet bun. She finished and grabbed her bag with her ballet slippers and tutu in it. She was already wearing her tights and leggings.

"Remember to put your coat on." mom told her as she ran down the stairs, "and don't dilly dally or you'll be late for ballet class."

"I won't Mom." Jeannie replied. Today was the first time she'd ever gone to ballet class on her own. Usually her mom took her and watched her classes but mom had joined a quilting club and today was their first gathering so Mom had told Jeannie that she was now old enough to take herself to her ballet lessons. Jeannie felt very grown up and proud to be going by herself. She was very excited.

Jeannie kissed her mom on the cheek and then ran out the door. She still had a little bit of time to get there. She'd actually left earlier than she normally had with her mom. Her mom had wanted her to have enough time to make it there on her own. "I'll just walk down past the pond on my way across the park." She told herself. She wouldn't really be dilly dallying. She still had lots of time, and she would make sure that she would not be late.

Two beautiful purple and green shining ducks were gliding along the water. They created two "v" patterns across the ripples. Then one ducked under the water so quickly that Jeannie had almost missed it. Then up it popped again, with a tiny little fish in its beak. It promptly lifted his head and opened its beak to swallow the little fish whole. The second duck then disappeared into the water and came back up again empty beaked. Off they swam creating another "v" pattern across the water.

Overhead, Jeannie looked up to see a similar 'v' pattern in the sky as a flock of Canadian geese flew past honking loudly. Jeannie smiled, trying to imagine what it must be like to fly over the mountains and lakes to make their way down south to the warm weather. Jeannie had to laugh again as she remembered the joke she'd heard today at school, "Why do geese fly south for the winter?" The reply being, "Because it's too far to walk!"

"Dong" Jeannie looked up at the library clock as it chimed.

"Oh, no, I'm late!" Jeannie exclaimed as she grabbed her bag and ran to her ballet class.

By the time she got there, the class had already warmed up and they were already working on their performance piece. "Oh Shoot!" It was too late to join the class. Her teacher, Miss Archer, wouldn't let any students join if they missed the warm-ups.

Jeannie slowly sat down on the bench to watch the rest of the class so she could at least learn the new routine as she watched. She wished desperately that she could join in. It sure wasn't fun sitting out.

Jeannie walked home slowly with her head hung low. She wished she had listened to her promise that she made to her mom that morning, and not dilly dallied at the pond. She promised herself that she would tell her mom the truth at dinner that she'd missed the class. Mom sure would be disappointed that Jeannie hadn't kept her promise.

At dinner, her mom asked, "So how was ballet class today?"

"Fine" Jeannie heard herself tell her mom, "Oh Shoot, now I've just lied to Mom" she thought to herself. Now how was she going to get out of this fix?

"So did you get to practice your attitude en pointe?" mom asked her. Mom knew she'd been working hard at getting her knee up just at the right angle while on her tippy-toe.

"Yeah, I still don't have the angle just right yet, but I'll keep at it," she again heard herself say. Why was she lying to her mom? It felt awful.

"Don't worry honey, you'll get it, I know you will." Mom smiled at her.

Jeannie heard her mom tell about her quilting session, but all she really wanted was to hurry up and finish dinner so she could go and hide in her room. It seemed to take ages but she finally found herself back in her room, after tidying up the dishes. She promised herself then and there, that next week she'd make sure she didn't dilly dally. She was definitely going to be on time!

Activity 1

Questions from the story

What was the promise that Jeannie had made to her mom before going to her ballet class?

What promise did Jeannie make to herself on her way to the park?

What two promises did she end up breaking?

When she broke the promises what happened at ballet class?

How did Jeannie feel about breaking her promises?

Because of her broken promise and her feeling, what did she end up doing at dinner?

How did that make her feel?

What was her new promise to herself for next week's class?

Do you think she will keep her promise?

Why do you think that?

Useful questions to ask your child and write down together

How have you broken your word?

How have you justified breaking your word?

How can you keep your word more often?

What do you want your word to be worth?

Activity 2

Make a list of your own broken promises as well as some promises that you can come up with that you might be able to see yourself making in the future. Then go over these broken promises and give some justification as to why you might break this promise. Then add some ways to help you avoid having to break these promises.

	Possible Broken Promises	What's Your Justification for Breaking Your Promise	How Can You Avoid Breaking this Promise?
1.			
2.			
3.			
4.			
5.			
6.			
7.			
8.			
9.			
10.			

Activity 3

Think back to your own life and share a story that relates to this topic, and discuss how you felt at their age, and what you learned from it.

"Be true to your work, your word, and your friend."
– Henry David Thoreau

---

6   Fear vs. Desire

*"Desire is creation, the magical element in that process.
If there were an instrument by which to measure desire,
one could foretell achievement."*
- Godfrey St. Peter

Humans are motivated by two factors, fear and desire. Although opposites of each other, they often work together. When your child does something, she is motivated by one or the other, and once in a while, by both. For example: you go to work to make money to be able to buy the things you want and need. The wanting is the desire; the needing is the fear of not having; not having a roof over your head, or enough food on the table. So you are motivated by both desire and fear to go to work.

So too is your child motivated. Let's take going to school as an example. She is motivated to go to school for possibly two reasons. Desire: she wishes to do well at school in order to get the positive attention from the teacher and also from you. Fear: she wants to go to school because she is afraid of letting you down or being suspended from school.

Sometimes your child will avoid something out of fear, like swimming away from a shark. However, fear isn't always this obvious. Your child may not consciously know that she even has a fear. She may just feel uncomfortable around a person or situation. Fear isn't a bad thing. In fact, it's often a great protector of your child. But fear can also hold her back from something she wants. This is one way where she may have conflicting intentions. She may want to make a new friend but is afraid of getting hurt. Maybe she's afraid that the person she wants to befriend won't like her. You can easily find out which is stronger, either her fear or her desire, by watching her end results. The results will tell the truth. She may have a really strong desire to befriend the new person. But if she doesn't go through with it, then the results clearly show that her fear of rejection is stronger than her desire of the pleasure of a new friendship.

Once you are able to show her the results of her actions then she may be able to finally let her fear go a little, and let her desire for the new friendship become the more powerful of the two. If her desire is more powerful than her fear, then she'll finally be able to create what she really wants. We are taught in schools that to fail is a bad thing. So her fear of being rejected is a very normal fear to have. Our job as parents is to show and coach our children that to fail is human. It's our way of learning and growing.

That rejection is in our minds. By not approaching the new friend, your child is already getting rejection from herself. We already have a "no," but by asking or reaching out for what we want we may just get a "yes." If we then still get a "no" we are no worse off than before. So encourage your child to go for the 'yes', she already has the "no," she can only stay the same or gain, she cannot in fact fail.

You may find that your child often has multiple intentions involved, and sorting through them all may take some time, especially if she doesn't even consciously know what her specific fears are. It can be helpful to recognize when fear shows up, so you help your child to consciously choose what she wants or how she can respond from a place of knowing. The simple way to get around this is to build up a clear intention of exactly what she does want. The key is being very specific and detailed as to stating what she wants. Does your child really know what she wants, or does she only know what she doesn't want? There is a huge difference between the two. In either case, it's most important to help your child get crystal clear on what she really wants.

You may notice that your child will try to avoid her fear by trying to change her outside environment, by changing classes, or changing after school activities or friends. However, even though she is changing her environment, she is not changing the fear inside, that lead her to the outside change. She is still carrying that same fear with her, and it will show its head again sometime in the future. You'll find that the change that she is looking for on the outside, will only actually happen once she makes the change on her inside. What we feel on the inside is reflected on the outside.

Try this with your child. Get a piece of paper and pen. Begin by having her imagine she has twenty million dollars, and whatever skills she needs can be taught to her. Also, let her know that she won't fail at whatever she chooses to do. Now, what does she want? Have her ask herself, "What do I want?" Have her be as detailed as possible. She should just write down whatever comes to her, no matter how weird it may sound. Keep asking her and have her just keep on writing down the ideas that come to her. Have her do this until she has filled at least one full page.

After she has written her list, have her go through each one, and write down how she will feel when she fulfills that desire. Have her write it as if she already has it. So for example, say she wants a new car, what kind? What color? What options? She could say something like, "I am riding my brand-new florescent pink, Trek bicycle down a bike trail in my favorite park with the warm breeze blowing through my hair." Say she wants to travel, where would she like to go? Who would she like to go with? For how long? Maybe she wants to make some new friends, or find that perfect boyfriend. How would they look? How would they make her feel? What kind of characteristics would they have? Have her paint a picture with her words. She needs to use action oriented adjectives and descriptive adverbs, like, "I'm happily attracting inspirational people to me daily through heartfelt communication."

Have your child do this for every aspect of her life. What she will get by doing this is empowerment. Your child's subconscious mind doesn't know the difference between pretending and reality. As far as it's concerned, both are "real." Your child's thoughts create her reality. There is a power in her word and more power still in her written word. Help your child to write at least a paragraph for each desire. Have her ask herself, what does she really want from each choice? Is she surprised by any of her desires? Are there any underlying wants that may not be directly connected to her desire? She may desire a place on the soccer team, for example, but really what she wants is to be able to have more friends and recognition that it will create. Can that be done with another way instead? Maybe or maybe not. The only way to find out is to explore the possibilities.

Maybe your child desires a new boyfriend, but really wants to be loved and supported. Can that be done in her present relationship? Again, maybe yes, maybe no. Asking her these kinds of questions will help her to sort out her desires. Your child has the choice to dream for anything. Why not have her paint a winning picture?

After all, it's her dream! Once she is clear about her desires, have her write them down and then put them where she can see them daily. If possible have her add photos that represent her desires. Then review them daily and watch them work!

"Our deepest fear is not that we are inadequate. Our deepest fear is that we are powerful beyond measure. It is our light not our darkness that most frightens us. We ask ourselves, who am I to be brilliant, gorgeous, talented, and fabulous? Actually, who are you not to be? You are a child of God. Your playing small does not serve the world. There is nothing enlightened about shrinking so that other people around you won't feel insecure. We were born to make manifest the glory of God that is within us. It is not just in some of us; it is in everyone. As we let our own light shine, we unconsciously give other people permission to do the same. As we are liberated from our own fear, our presence automatically liberates others."
– Marianne Williamson

Story: Scottie's PERFECT DAY Finally Arrives

"I can't believe I did that!" Scottie exclaimed to Suzy as he sat next to her on the bus ride home. "Did what?" Suzy asked.

"Oh Suzy, I'd counted so much on winning the speech contest in English class. I really wanted the first prize. Mrs. Kneedock had arranged for the winner of the speeches to get to go to the zoo. She has a family pass for the zoo." Scottie moaned.

"But Scottie, the zoo is only 15 minutes from here, you could go anytime." Suzy was confused. "You don't understand Suzy, my parents always say that we'll go, but we never do. Something else always comes up. It's not about the zoo, Suzy. We never do anything together as a family. I can see that my little brother, Tommy, is really missing them. They are always so busy. I remember going to the circus, or the park, or just to the mall with them. But we've not done something like that in a very long time. Tommy's so little that he doesn't even remember doing anything as a family. I want him to have some fun family memories too." Scottie explained.

"But how would winning a family pass to the zoo help, if your parents are always busy?" Suzy asked.

"Don't you see, Suzy, if I won a family pass that had an expiration date on it, then they would have to make time. They wouldn't waste the ticket, I know it. They are always saying, 'waste not, want not.' So I know that if I had won that pass then we would go and Tommy could start to build some fun family memories."

"Oh I see. I am sorry it didn't work out for you" said Suzy, "what happened in class today?" "Oh, don't ask." Scottie said under his breath.

"No, Scottie, let's look at it. Let's figure out what happened. Maybe there's a way around it." Suzy encouraged.

"No way around it, Suzy. It's over now. The vote will be in tomorrow morning. It's all on camera and we're going to review the speeches tomorrow morning and then vote on the winner. I'm out. That's that. There is nothing more I can do." Scottie was discouraged.

"So, tell me already, what happened?" Suzy was getting impatient. "Alright, if you must know…"

"I must!" Suzy interrupted.

Scottie continued, "It was going really well. I did what you said to do about writing out my 'Perfect Day'. I said how happy I was that I won the speech and won the family pass. I wrote it all out in detail. I spent weeks on preparing my speech, I made sure I put in lots of sensory words and lots of interesting facts and I even had diagrams and charts to show. It was really great." Scottie seemed prouder.

"So what happened?" Suzy encouraged.

"I walked up to the front of the class, took a deep breath… and then I froze!" Scottie admitted, "It was horrifying. I was so embarrassed. I went completely blank. All those weeks of practicing went out the window. I couldn't remember a single thing. Everyone started to snicker. I couldn't even move. It was the worst moment of my life. I could actually see the gates of the zoo being shut closed right in front of my family.

We were sent away. It was truly awful. I never want to do that again, ever!" Scottie exclaimed.

"Oh Scottie, I'm so sorry that happened. I'm sure it was truly awful. I hate to say this, but do you know what?" Suzy prodded.

"What?" Scottie's embarrassment was slowly fading away again. "I bet you still got what you really wanted." Suzy stated.

"Suzy! How can you say that? I thought you were my friend." Scottie could feel the heat rise in his cheeks. How dare she? She was supposed to be on his side. So much for confiding in her! He sure wouldn't do that again. Scottie was about to stand up and find another seat. He didn't have to put up with this.

Suzy put out her hand to stop him, "Sit down Scottie. I'm on your side." Scottie sat down again reluctantly.

"No really, let's go over it in detail. Sometimes we think we want something, that's called our 'desire' but we actually deep down inside have a stronger 'fear' that will never let us get what we want. I'm not the one who's against you, you are. Don't you see you can only attract to you what you really want? No one else is ever to blame. So somewhere deep inside there must have been a conflicting idea or 'fear' that was stronger than your 'desire'. Let's figure it out." Suzy explained.

"You're talking all confusing again Suzy." Scottie injected.

"Trust me on this Scottie. I've done it myself so many times I can't even count them anymore, but I have learned that somewhere deep inside of me must be an even stronger opposing fear to my outside desire. Think back. What exactly did you imagine when you imagined winning the family pass. What did you say to yourself?" Suzy asked.

"Well, I told myself how happy I was now that I had won the family pass to the zoo. I saw myself being given the pass by my teacher and the whole class clapping." Scottie told her.

"Okay, great, you're on the right track, who knows that may even still happen." Suzy encouraged.

"No way, I told you already I missed my opportunity the voting is tomorrow morning." Scottie said.

"Don't worry about that. The law of attraction can do anything." She stated. "What you attract you will get. It's really that simple. So let's continue. Tell me how you felt when you imagined yourself standing in front of the class doing your speech." Suzy asked.

"Oh I didn't spend much time on that at all. Every time I imagined myself in front of the class I would get a horrible hard ball in my stomach, I could imagine everyone laughing at me so I just focused on getting the pass instead." Scottie admitted.

"See, Scottie, your opposing fear of being laughed at may have gotten in the way of you getting your desire, the family pass to the zoo." Suzy pointed out.

"Yes, I'm beginning to see that." Scottie said.

"Here's our stop," Suzy said, gathering her bag, "I'll come over tonight and we can re-write your 'desire' to get the family pass, okay?"

"What's the use?" Scottie said, walking down the aisle "It can't happen anymore anyway, it's over." "A dream is never over," Suzy stated.

They got off the bus and went their separate ways. "I'll be over in ten minutes" Suzy yelled.

Scottie smiled to himself as he walked into his English class the next morning. It had felt really great going over his dreams last night with Suzy. She's made him rewrite his goal of getting the family pass to the zoo. She had made sure that he wrote down all of the details especially including how he felt. He'd written how wonderfully proud and happy he felt as his whole class clapped wildly for him as his teacher handed him the family pass. He wrote all about the day at the zoo with his family; which animals they would visit, where they would sit down at lunch. He even imagined wiping a finger print off of the glass of the underwater polar bear exhibition. He smiled again as he thought of that.

At first he'd felt silly writing this all out when the speeches were already over and he knew he couldn't win the pass from his English class. But Suzy had insisted on doing it anyway, she said that who knew, it may happen in the future, who are we to argue with the law of attraction? She'd had a point so he went into it whole heartedly and had really enjoyed the exercise.

"Good morning Scottie," Mrs. Kneedock greeted him. "Good morning" he replied.

As he sat down in his desk, Mrs. Kneedock announced to the class that there had been a problem with the video recorder yesterday and the last two speeches had not been recorded. She asked the last two students if they wanted to do theirs again. It was up to them. Scottie felt the fear rage through his body. He'd been the last one. What should he do?

"Paulie, would you like to do yours again? You don't have to, we can remember your speech without the playback but you may if you like." Mrs. Kneedock asked the first missed student.

"No thank-you Mrs. Kneedock, I'd rather not" Scottie heard Paulie reply.

"That's okay Paulie, how about you Scottie? Would you like to redo your speech?" Scottie could hear the stillness in the room as everyone waited in anticipation of what Scottie would do.

"Just do it!" a voice from deep inside came up. "This is your chance" it continued. "Do this or you won't be able to face Suzy after school." The voice was right.

"Okay, Mrs. Kneedock, I'll do mine again." Scottie stood up and walked to the front of the class. He turned to the group and began, "Good morning every one, today I want to talk to you about poison ivory..." the heat rushed immediately up to his face. He'd said it wrong. He was supposed to be talking about poison ivy, not ivory. He heard a few giggles and felt himself freeze to the spot. He couldn't do it. He knew that he'd let Suzy down but he just couldn't do it.

After a few more minutes, Mrs. Kneedock walked over to Scottie and placed her hand on his shoulder, "It's okay, Scottie, you may sit down. Thank-you for trying."

Scottie sat down and put his head on his table. He'd flopped again! He couldn't believe it. Suzy was wrong, he couldn't just write down his goals to make them come true. It was no use.

They spent the rest of the morning going over yesterday's speeches and then wrote their votes. "You'll be voting on which speech you enjoyed the most." Mrs. Kneedock said.

The votes were collected. A few minutes later Mrs. Kneedock announced that Patti Hamsburg had won the speech competition. She handed the happy girl her family pass to the zoo. Everyone clapped. She was a sight to see, she was so happy. Scottie clapped for her as well, and tried to be a good sport about it. She did deserve it. He'd voted for her himself. She'd been amazing. Her speech on how you could ride on the crest of a wave on your stomach had been incredible. Everyone had wanted to rush outside to the nearest beach to give it a try.

"Okay class," Mrs. Kneedock interrupted the clapping, "I have one more family pass to hand out." Everyone stopped clapping and there was an instant hush in the room. They all wanted it but Scottie knew he wouldn't get it. He hadn't even been able to get past his first sentence. He was curious to see who else would get the pass.

"By a show of hands, I'd like to have you tell me who you would like to have the second family pass. This pass will be going to the person who had the most obstacles to overcome. I'd like to call this pass the "good sport" pass. Okay, any suggestions?" she asked the class.

Immediately a few hands went up.

"Okay, Brian, who would you like to nominate?" she asked.

"I think Betty Sue should get it, she had to climb over a fence that had a guard dog to get to her interview with the dog lady for her speech. That took some guts." He said.

The class nodded in agreement but there were still more hands up.

"Okay, that is very good Brian. We sure are proud of you Betty Sue for going that extra mile" she admired. "Josephine, who would you like to nominate?" she asked.

"I think Scottie should get it," Scottie was shocked to hear his own name, "he had the hardest time of all of us. First he froze on the spot. Then the recorder didn't even record that, and then he had to do it all again! I really admire him for trying the second time. I sure wouldn't have gone up to do that again. I think he's the real 'good sport' of our class." She said.

All the other hands went down immediately.

"Yeah, she's right!" Betty Sue yelled out. "He deserves it more than I do. I climbed over the fence but the lady had already put the dog in his kennel so there was no real danger, even if I didn't know about it. Scottie deserves it." She insisted.

"Yea! Scottie, Scottie, Scottie," the class started to chant.

"I guess that says it then," Mrs. Kneedock exclaimed. She walked over to Scottie, "please accept this family pass to the zoo from us, your class, for choosing you as our 'good sport' speaker." She handed Scottie the pass.

Scottie couldn't believe what was happening. It was all coming to life just like in his statement. The class burst out into unbelievably supportive and loud clapping and cheers. Everyone stood up. Scottie could see clearly that they were clapping for him, not laughing at him. They really wanted him to win. It was incredible! It was just like in his script. They all stood up and continued to clap. Some were even stamping their feet to the rhythm. Scottie felt wonderful inside, he couldn't wait to take his family to the zoo. His little brother would have the time of his life. Scottie graciously accepted the pass and everyone cheered. He smiled, "I can't wait to tell Suzy about this," he thought.

Activity 1

Questions from the story

What was Scottie's fear that at first overpowered his desire?

What feeling did Scottie have that made him freeze in front of the class?

Whos fault was it that Scottie froze?

What key advice did Suzy give to help Scottie re-write his intention?

How did Scottie feel inside about his re-written intention?

Why was Scottie still not able to do his speech?

Did his not being able to say his speech have any effect on the outcome of his dream?

What lesson did Scottie learn about the law of attraction?

Useful questions to ask your child and write down together

What have I been truly afraid of?

Are any of these fears real and valid?

What do I really desire in my life?

Who's really in charge of your future, the getting of your dreams?

Activity 2

Go back to your 'perfect day' and choose 5 of your most important desires and write out in absolute detail the precise description of the end result of your goals. As with Scottie, it didn't matter that he failed at the speech, he still won his goal. And that is also true with your life. You may not be in control of how you receive your goals but you are in control of how you will feel once you get those goals. It's important to remember that you can only decide your outcomes and you have no right to choose another's outcome.

So for example, say you had a dream to be on the Oprah Winfrey show. You are not allowed to say, "I'm so happy and grateful now that I've been interviewed on Opera." She has free will as well as you and she may choose whether or not she would like to interview you. You have no right to force your dream on someone else. However, you have the absolute right to say something like, "I'm so happy and grateful now that I am constantly interviewed on shows like the Opera Winfrey Show." By saying the word, "like" you are opening up your possibilities, the right show for you will come along and you are not putting your dreams on anyone else, they too will have chosen to interview someone like you.

"Desire is half of life, indifference is half of death."
– Kahlil Gibran

Your Top 5 Dreams/Goals	Describe Your End Result in Absolute Detail	Describe How this Result Will Make You Truly Feel
1.		
2.		
3.		
4.		
5.		

Activity 3

Think back to your own life and share a story that relates to this topic, and discuss how you felt at their age, and what you learned from it

7   How to Change Your Child's Mind

"Like all weak men, he laid an exaggerated stress on not changing one's mind."
– W. Somerset Maugham

Don't you agree that having your child waste their mind is a terrible thing? You're right! More specifically, having your child NOT use their mind is a terrible waste. We all use some of our minds abilities, and we all use more of our subconscious mind than we even realize. For example, have you ever driven somewhere and after you did so wonder how you got there because, you weren't paying attention? In cases like this, your subconscious mind drove you. Luckily, we have a very powerful and talented subconscious mind. And so does your child!

Your child doesn't have to remember how to brush their teeth, they may have to be reminded to do it, but once they know how, they will always remember that. The same goes for talking, eating, walking, and any number of other repetitive things that we've learned. Once you teach your child how to do these things, they will always remember them. Our subconscious mind knows, remembers, and does so many things for us. There's a great expression most of us know that describes this beautifully, "It's like riding a bike," which means that once you've learned to ride, that knowledge will still be there, forever. It may be frustrating at times having the patience to teach your child all of the things that they will need to know in order to survive in the world, but rest assured that once they have learned them, they will always have that knowledge.

Okay now, you may think that your child only uses his basic subconscious mind but in reality he uses his subconscious mind daily for much more than you may know. Let's say he meets someone and he 'feels' good about them, it's his subconscious mind at work. Or let's say he is hoping for something and by 'coincidence' that thing shows up, it's his subconscious mind at work.

He has actually been creating his life as he goes along. Sometimes there's more than just his mind at work in this creative process. Just know that we are all capable of creating lots of things in our lives. It's important for your child to know what he is creating, so if he wants something else, he needs to make sure he has one clear intention, and releases any competing ones.

Unless it's something new that he wants. If he doesn't have it, he probably has a competing intention, or belief, that has kept him from getting what he wants. On a good note, sometimes we actually get something better than what we want! As long as he's okay with 'better', it works for him. However, if for some reason, he has a limiting belief about something, even if he gets it, he'll probably lose it, unless he changes his belief. Sometimes he might have a 'goodness' ceiling. Once he hits that level of 'goodness', of things going his way, or good fortune, he will subconsciously sabotage himself to keep himself 'safe' in his comfort zone. Ask him how good can he stand himself to feel? Have you ever noticed how many lottery winners lose all of it within five years? It's because they went far out of their comfort zone, and sabotaged themselves until they returned to it.

He may sometimes fear failure, even success, and many times, it's on a subconscious level. What he believes on a conscious level may not agree with his subconscious level. The important thing is, does he like what he's getting? As Dr. Phil McGraw says, "How's that working for you?" Assuming he wants something different than he has, does he consciously feel he deserves it? If he does, and he doesn't have it, is he really clear about what it is that he wants? What if he were to tell you, "I want more money!?" Will twenty-five cents be enough for him? That's more money, after all.

His intentions or goals need to be S.M.A.R.T. (Specific, Measurable, Appropriate, Realistic, and have a finite measurement of Time.) Take Specific for example. How much more money would your child really want? When he says, "I want to have a brand new website on convertible cars that brings in $2,000, by the end of this year," that's specific. It's also measurable.

Appropriate has to do with several factors. Does it meet your child's needs and wants? Does it interfere with someone else's? Think of the interference like this, "I want Mary to be my girlfriend," versus, "I want to have a loving, romantic relationship with someone like Mary." He can ask to have a girlfriend like Mary, but whether or not that person will actually be Mary is uncertain. As far as intentions go, Mary has a life of her own. She has her own choice to be with someone like your son or not to be. By asking for someone like Mary to be his girlfriend, whether or not he ends up with Mary is irrelevant, the fact is he will end up with someone like her and will be totally satisfied with that! He may get what he wants, or he may get even better, so it's best for him not to limit himself.

Realistic is a little more of a grey area. Realistic is about believability, your child's believability with his goal. A good rule of thumb is to have him make his intention fifty percent believable or fifty percent unbelievable, whichever works for him. So if making $1,000 on the internet with his own website is believable by the end of the year, then $2,000 is fifty percent believable. $50,000 is not realistic, at least not in one year. In two and a half years, however, it could be realistic. It could still happen, but stretching his reality and his comfort zone to that level might be more challenging.

There is a reasonable finite measurement of Time to this goal as well, so we have all the elements. Try it yourself with various parts of your life. See if you change your mind, and start getting what you want.

You can use these goals as guideposts to keep you and your child on track. If you find that either one of you is off, just adjust your efforts or goals to fit.

Whenever you make a goal, be sure to add "This or something better for my highest good." at the end. If you have a choice, why limit yourself by your vision, instead let your dreams be unlimited!

"The secret of getting ahead is getting started.
The secret of getting started is breaking your complex overwhelming tasks into small manageable tasks, and then starting on the first one."
– Mark Twain

Story: Annie Gets Something Even Better Than What She Wants

"Annie, wait up!" Marcy yelled as she chased her friend down. "What happened in there?"

"Oh, I don't want to talk about it Marcy" Annie said sullenly. She'd just been so embarrassed by Kevin. She had asked him to the Halloween dance and he had not only refused, but he had been downright rude about it.

"Oh come on Annie," Marcy insisted. "What did he say?"

"He said, he would rather go to the dance with a cage full of bats than go with me. It was so awful Marcy." The tears started streaming down her face as they walked down the sidewalk. Marcy lived two doors down from Annie and had been her best friend since their moms first bumped into each other while walking them in their baby carriages twelve years earlier.

"It couldn't have been that bad," Marcy tried to make her feel better but it wasn't working.

"Oh, Marcy, I thought I'd picked just the right moment. Kevin had been all alone in the hall, so I thought, and so I asked him, and then I heard snickering coming from around the corner and then Bill walked in on us. Kevin started to get all funny and then he said those awful things. He could have just said no. He didn't have to be so mean."

"They're such idiots!" Marcy was a true best friend sticking up for her in her time of need.

"I don't care anyway, I'm just going to stay home on Halloween, I don't need the embarrassment" Annie said.

"No you don't Annie! You're going to go with me!"
"Don't make me laugh" Annie started to smile a little.

"I mean it," said Marcy, "who says you can't just go with your best friend, I don't think it's written somewhere that you have to go with a guy!"

"But you already promised you'd go with Sam, or did you forget?" Annie asked.

"Oops! Don't tell him. But I'm sure he wouldn't mind if you came with us." Marcy insisted. "No way!" Annie was not going to do that!

"We'll figure something out, don't worry Annie." Marcy waved goodbye to her friend and turned in at her gate.

Annie turned down her own driveway a few meters away and could hear the TV blaring from inside. "Oh great, mom's home" she said to herself. Mom would want to know how it went. She knew Annie was going to ask Kevin to the dance. She took a deep breath and went inside.

"Hi honey, is that you? Come in here, I want you to see this." Her mom yelled out as she closed the door and took off her jacket.

"What is it, Mom? I could hear it all the way down the street." Annie exaggerated.

"Oh, is it that loud, here I'll turn it down a little. My friend, Marita came over this afternoon and left this with me. She insisted l leave my chores and watch this right away. She was right, this is important. Come have a look." Mom called out.

"Okay, okay, I'm coming." Annie slowly made her way into the family room. She could hear strange music and a narrator coming out of the TV set. "So what is it Mom?"

"It's called "The Secret" it's incredible. I want to try it out right away, but I'll rewind it and you can have a look at it with me," Mom said excitedly.

"Do I have to Mom? It looks odd and I have homework." Annie tried to get out of it.

"No honey, sit down, this is important. So what did Kevin say? Is he taking you to the dance?" Mom asked.

"No" was Annie short reply. She braced herself for the next question but it didn't come. "No worries Annie," she heard her mother say. "Watch this with me, maybe it will help."

How a TV movie would help her get Kevin to take her to the Halloween dance was beyond her, but she knew there was no use in arguing with her mom. Once her mom made up her mind about something she would bug you until you did it, so it would be easier to just sit down and watch the dumb movie and get it over with.

She made herself comfortable next to her mom on the couch and started to watch the movie. After about ten minutes she was in awe. "Wow! If these people could do this then surely she could." Annie thought to herself. Mom had been right, this movie was great! Although, it wasn't really a movie it was more of a documentary. It was all about what they called, "the law of attraction" and it showed story after story of how all of these different people had created the future they wanted for themselves by using the way they thought. It seemed too good to be true. But they even had a man on there that had had a terrible accident and wasn't even expected to live. Even if he did live, he was expected to be a vegetable for the rest of his life. Instead, he had decided to work on his mindset. He decided to walk out of the hospital all on his own before Christmas, which had only been a few months away. It was an impossible task and yet he had done it.

If someone like him could get his entire life back when he had been completely paralyzed and expected to be a vegetable for the rest of his life; then surely she could get something as simple as having Kevin take her to the dance.

"Thanks Mom, you're right. This is great! I'm going to my room to write out my perfect day for the dance right now. I'll help make dinner in a little while okay?" She asked as she already started to run up the stairs to her room.

"That's fine honey" she heard her mom reply as she shut her bedroom door.

"Hey idiot, get out of my way" Kevin bellowed at Annie as she stumbled out of the way. She hadn't seen them coming through the school doors, and she nearly lost all of her books in the process.

Well, things weren't working out like she had planned. It was so disappointing. She could see that there was no way that Kevin was going to change his mind. Even though she had spent all of her time before and after dinner last night writing out how wonderful the dance was now that she was there with Kevin on her arm.

She couldn't see how it would work. Kevin was being just as rude to her as usual. She'd done everything they'd told her to do in the movie. She'd written all about the end result, not wasting time on how to get there. It was just writing about how she felt when she walked in the gym door with Kevin on her arm. It sent wonderful chills all up her body. She's written the exact details of how she would dress, how Kevin would look, how it would feel to be dancing together for their first dance. The way Kevin would put his arm around her and even what song would be playing as they ended the dance with a gentle kiss. But as far as she could see, it was all a hoax. There was no way that she could imagine him going to the dance with her. He'd been just downright rude and mean to her every chance she'd seen him.

"It's useless!"

"What's useless?" Marcy asked her.

Annie hadn't realized that she's spoken out loud. She restacked her books and walked down the hall with Marcy to put her books in her locker for lunch.

"Oh nothing" Annie tried to shrug it off.

"Come on Annie," Marcy encouraged. "What's useless? It must be something for you to say it like that."

"Oh all right. I was watching this movie with mom after school yesterday and it was all about the 'law of attraction' and…"

"What's that?" Marcy interrupted.

"Oh, it's a natural law that says that we attract into our lives the thoughts that we send out. So if we want to have good things happen to us then we need to send out good thoughts of how they will happen and so on." Annie briefly explained.

"Cool!" Marcy was intrigued. "Does it really work? Sounds like magic. So if I want an apple pie for dinner tonight, I just think of it?"

"Something like that." Annie said.

"So is it working for you? Oh wait, I just heard you say, 'it's useless', was that what you were thinking about?" Marcy asked.

"Yeah, I spent all night writing out how Kevin was still going to take me to the dance and he's just been a real bully to me all day. So I don't know how that guy managed to walk out of the hospital when he was going to be a vegetable all his life…"

"He what? Who is this guy? What are you talking about?" Marcy looked confused. "Oh, sorry, Marcy, I'll explain it all while we have lunch." Annie quickly explained.

"Are you sure you want to go to a dance with Kevin, if he treats you this way? First of all, you deserve better than that Annie and besides, do you really believe he will go with you?" Marcie asked.

"Not really, but this Movie said all I have to do is write it down, so I want to see if it will work." Annie insisted.

"All right, Annie. Good luck then." Marcie shrugged her shoulders. Annie could seed that Marcie thought she was out of her mind. Marcie just didn't know that Kevin was really nice deep down inside. Marcie just didn't see it. But Annie knew he really was nice, he just didn't want everyone to know, that's all.

"For now let's just say that I'm obviously missing a key ingredient in this law of attraction stuff." Annie smiled at her friend.

"Hey Mom, where's that movie we watched yesterday?" Annie yelled out as she entered her house. "Hi honey, what's that?" her mom asked poking her head out of the laundry room.

"The movie, "The Secret", I have to see it again, I think I missed something." Annie explained.

"Sure honey, it's still in the DVD player, I haven't given it back yet. Marita is coming to pick it up after dinner she wanted to show it to her brother, who's just lost his job." Her mom said.

"Oh good, it's still here. I have to see it. I'll catch you later mom" Annie hurried to the TV.

Annie couldn't tear her eyes from the screen. How had she missed this vital piece of the law of attraction puzzle? She was so grateful that she'd figured it out.

"Wow you look amazing!" Marcy greeted Annie at her gate. "Yeah, Annie, you look great!"

"Thanks Sam, you two don't look so bad yourselves." Annie teased them. She'd decide to go with them to the dance. She knew that her vision would still come true, even if Kevin hadn't asked her to the dance in the end. She had conceived the idea. She absolutely believed it would happen, and so now she was open and relaxed and excited to receive her dream. Kevin didn't know what was coming! She smiled to herself. All would be just fine.

"So how did your goal go Annie?" Marcy asked as they entered the gym at the dance.

Just then Annie noticed a new boy getting out of a friend's car. He looked at Annie and smiled. She smiled back.

"It's going great!" Annie said excitedly.

"But what was the secret ingredient? You didn't tell me." Marcy complained.

Annie gave her a smile and said, "Marcy, the key is that YOU can have anything YOU want, but you CAN'T FORCE others to have what they DON'T want."

"Huh?" Marcy was confused. "But you wanted Kevin to take you to the dance. He's not, and you still look happy, I don't get it."

"I learned that I am not allowed, none of us are allowed, to put our goals on others. Everyone has to make their own goals. So instead of writing that 'I was so happy and grateful that Kevin had taken me to the dance,' I change it to 'I'm so happy and grateful that someone LIKE Kevin had taken me to the dance. And I also learned that I had to really believe my goal was possible. Deep down I know that Kevin will never go with me to a dance." Annie explained.

"But you're here with us, not someone like Kevin, so why are you so happy?" Marcy was totally confused.

"Because I am here with you AND someone LIKE Kevin, only WAY BETTER!" with that Annie, smiled and waved goodbye and walked over to the new kid and she put her arm through his extended one.

Marcy just stared with her mouth dropped open.

"I'd like to introduce you to Mike," Annie said to Marcy as she sauntered past Marcy and Sam. "He's the nephew of my mom's friend, Marita. He's moving to our area, and will be going to our school. We met last night. So I asked him to come to the dance after he got back from his old school."

"And I immediately said yes. Who could resist an invitation like that! Hi I'm Mike. Pleased to meet you both. Annie has told me all about you." Mike held out his hand to shake theirs.

Marcy gave him a bewildered shake of her hand.

"Wow, the law of attraction..." Annie heard Marcy whisper under her breath. Annie took hold of Mike's arm and spying Kevin looking at her, proudly paraded her group into the dance.

Activity 1

Questions from the story

Why didn't Annie's first attempt at writing her future work?

What was the missing ingredient or 'key' that Annie forgot to write down in her dream?

Why is it important to use words like, "someone like" instead of just writing the person down who your dream/goal is about?

Is anyone allowed to put you in their goals?

What happened once Annie put the words, "someone like" into her script? What was the second key?

What do you think Marcie thought of Annie wanting to go to the dance with Kevin, when he treated her the way he did?

Would you want to go to a dance with someone who treats you that way?

The person who Annie did end up going to the dance with ended up to be even 'better' than Kevin, in which way do you think he was 'better' for Annie?

Useful questions to ask your child and write down together

What are my intentions?

Do I have any competing intentions? If so, what are they?

What do I believe about me?

Am I putting other people into my goals?

Will I get better results if I change them to 'someone like'?

Do my goals meet the S.M.A.R.T criteria?

Activity 2

Go back to your top 5 goals that you wrote out in Chapter 6. First go through each one to see if you have any competing intentions that may stop you from achieving that goal. Then go through each one and see if they are S.M.A.R.T. (Note: Make sure that if any of your goals includes another person, you write the words, "someone like" in front of their names so you don't infringe on their own free will.)

Goal or Possible Competing Intention	Specific What Do You Want, Exactly?	Measurable Exactly How Much Do You Want?	Appropriate Does it Meet Your Needs? Does It Interfere With Anyone Else's Needs?	Realistic Is it 50% Believable for YOU?	Time By When Do You Want This to Happen?
1.					
2.					
3.					
4.					
5.					

Activity 3

Think back to your own life and share a story that relates to this topic, and discuss how you felt at their age, and what you learned from it.

"To think is to create"
– Napoleon Hill

8   Helping Your Child to Take Back Their Power

"Everything can be taken from a man but...the last of the human freedoms—to choose one's attitude in any given set of circumstances, to choose one's own way."
– Viktor E. Frankl

Your child may not even realize the power that she has to create the life she wants, even if she is willing to use it. She may feel powerless when life sometimes presents her with events, which she has no control in bringing about. As we discussed earlier about having intentions, she creates her own life. How she creates her life is up to her. Sometimes she may really want something and she doesn't end up creating it. Like the words from a Garth Brooks song, "Unanswered Prayers," she may discover later that sometimes there was something better that she didn't even consciously know about. Only afterwards will she be able to look back and see that it was better. What you have to help your child realize is, there is a bigger picture, and she is sometimes too close to see the whole picture. Like a puzzle, as she adds the pieces, she will get a better idea of what she's creating. This is one of those pieces. How your child puts the pieces of her life together is up to her.

One thing that can keep your child from connecting to her power is addictions. Addictions have their own agenda, and it's in direct opposition to her power. Addictions run from the classic substance addiction, to the behavioral. Your child may be addicted to the TV or the internet. Often behavioral addictions aren't recognized or acknowledged. Regardless of what your child may use to avoid reality, it does have a cost. Making decisions when under the influence of her addiction is usually not for her highest good. When your child is under the influence, her guilt center is removed temporarily, and replaced with the "I want" mechanism. The "I want" could be most anything depending on the addiction. The bottom line will be, "I want to satisfy my needs," which include feeding the addiction, and any other "self-medicating" behavior that makes her "feel safe." This often makes her "feel nothing," that is, numbing her emotions. This is why overweight people eat, even when they're full. They are "looking for love in all the wrong places." They are literally trying to satisfy their need for love and safety.

Addiction is not dealing with reality. Its answer may only satisfy your child for the moment, and sometimes not even then. It's a response of feeling "out of control." That is, your child may feel, "I don't have the ability to control getting what I want." That is the basic error, believing that she doesn't have the ability to get what she needs. Helping your child to believe that she can change is the key to creating her dreams. She does have the power to change. You have to show your child that she has the responsibility. Therefore, your child has the ability to choose how she responds! That's the good news! Your child can create something different than what she presently has. But she needs to choose differently than she has chosen in her past.

You may notice that your child may cling sometimes to the status quo for fear of the unknown. This is often what has kept us stuck. We'd rather keep what we know, even though we don't like it, than what we don't know. That is when fate steps in. When we need to move forward in life, but refuse, a crisis comes along. A crisis is a gift, although it often may seem just the opposite at first. A crisis is an opportunity for transforming your child's life. A crisis takes your child out of her comfort zone. She gets caught up in blaming. Lots of "shoulds" come up, like, "It should be different. It should be better. I shouldn't have to deal with this."

The real challenge for your child is fear. When she can face her fears, she can create the life that she really wants.

Getting your child to move through her fear is the key to having her get what she wants. Fear can be a valuable and useful part of life, but sometimes, your child may use it as a reason to hold herself back in her life. How she chooses to relate to fear will determine how she'll create her reality. Don't let her let fear stop her from getting what she really wants. Instead, have your child focus on what she wants.

Explain to her how she has the choice. She can choose to put the energy on the goal she wants, or on her fear. It's her choice. The energy will go to one of them, so she may as well consciously choose the object of her focus. She will then find that the more she focuses on her goal, the less power fear will have on her.

Having your child take back her power means to claim her life for what she wants it to be. Help your child to start taking back her power by having her take responsibility for her life. Remember, to claim responsibility, claims her power. She has the ability to change her life.

It's up to your child to make the choice to change. But you can help her to see that it is her own choice. Once she sees this, and makes the decision to change; her life will shift. She doesn't even need to know how to make it happen. She just needs to have a clear vision of what she really wants. This will come from her heart, not her head. Only your child can keep herself from getting what she really wants. Once she is in alignment with her heart, her life will move forward and everything she needs, will show up.

If you find that your child is still having trouble getting in touch with what it is that she really wants, get her to try to take time to sit and be quiet with the intention of having what she really wants come to her. It's amazing how effective this can be. Have her do this daily if you can. Once she has a clear picture of what she really wants, have her close her eyes. Get your child to imagine she has already achieved her goals. Have her really feel what it feels like. How is she feeling? How is she being different?

Encourage her to remember how it feels, and how she is being.

One really good activity to do with your child is to begin with each day having your child take a few minutes of "remembering" the feeling that she created with her having achieved her goal. Have her sit quietly and just focus her attention on this feeling as if it were true now. Watch how she is being shifted to match this. It will happen. Her mind will make it so.

"It often takes a crisis to break through our usual models of the world. A crisis is a gift, an opportunity, and perhaps a manifestation that life loves us, by beckoning us to go beyond the dance we presently perform."
– Leslie Lebeau

Story: Nat Conquers Her Fear

"I just can't do it!" Nat declared.

"Natalie Stewart, you are not a quitter!" Mrs. Lovington stated.

"But Mrs. Lovington, I just can't. I'll fall again. It took me six weeks to finally get the cast off my arm. I'm afraid I'll break it again." Nat said.

"Nat, that was two months ago. Your arm is back to health, the doctors say you may use it normally again. You're letting your fear determine your future." Mrs. Lovington was firm in her remark.

"But what if I fall again, if I break it again, I may never get to do gymnastics again." Natalie pleaded.

"Well, it's up to you Nat. It's your future. If you want to be a gold medal gymnast then you will have to get past this fear. If you let your fear guide you then you won't get to realize your dream anyway. So it's up to you Nat." Mrs. Lovington continued to be firm.

Mrs. Lovington had been Nat's high school gymnastics coach for over three years now. Nat had been doing really well under her leadership. She was an excellent floor gymnast. She could spin higher than anyone else in the school. She had been very confident on the balance beam as well until this recent fall.

Nat had been trying a new move. She'd wanted to do a jump/twist/back-flip on the beam and then bounce up from that and twirl her way off the beam for her dismount. It had all gone so well. She had jumped high on the beam, did her twist in the air into her back flip, landed on the beam and had bounced high for her last twirl off of the beam when she came down she had misjudged her distance from the end of the beam by a hair and that had caused her to land off balance and crash down onto the ground, missing the safety mat and crushing her left arm under her. She'd had two breaks in her lower arm. It had been a tremendous pain and had taken months to finally heal well enough for her to be able to start using it again.

The doctors had said that she would be fine; she just needed to be careful with it and go gently at first until her arm muscle had built up enough again to take on its own support.

Mrs. Lovington was right, she was capable to do her work again, since she could easily bear most of her weight on her right arm to give her left arm the chance it needed to strengthen up again but a terrible fear of the fall constantly played in Nat's mind and she was terrified of having it happen again.

"I really do want to be a gold medalist for gymnastics" Nat insisted to her coach.

"You know what Nat," her coach soothed, "sometimes you just need to feel the fear and do it anyway." "I know, you always tell me that."

"Well, it's very true." Her coach said.

"But how can I do the balance beam when every time I get close to it I feel like I'm about to throw up?" Nat asked.

"Well, if this is really your dream then you will do anything it takes to build up your courage. It's really that simple. Maybe there is a lesson in this. Have you gone over in your mind why you missed your mark, when you fell?" Mrs. Lovington questioned.

"I don't know. I hadn't thought about that." Nat answered.

"We attract everything in our life to us Nat. So somewhere in your past you must have had some thought that brought you to this." Mrs. Lovington said.

"You mean, you're saying that I purposely hurt myself? Get real. I want the gold; I'm not going to sabotage that." Nat was indignant.

"All I'm saying is that somewhere something happened that made you lose your concentration. Figure out what it was and then you may be able to get past this," said her coach.

Nat went over to the bench to sit down and think about this. This was ridiculous. But since there was no way she was going back up on the balance beam right now she figured she may as well see if she could figure this out.

Did she really want the gold medal? Yeah! So then why was she afraid to get back up and practice?

That was easy! She didn't want to break her arm again. But if she didn't practice then she would never achieve her dream. So what if she never became a top gymnast? Did it really matter to her?

Nat thought and thought. But she really couldn't see her life going any other direction. Well, she could be a coach, she consoled herself. She knew enough to be that! But then what kind of coach would she be if she herself had given up when the going got tough?

Oh, she just didn't know!

Nat could see Mrs. Lovington coming her way again. She tried to be invisible, she didn't want another discussion.

"Nat," her coach said as she sat down next to her on the bench, "I don't mean to be hard on you or to discourage you. I truly can see that you are my best student. You really have the potential to get the gold medal. But you won't get it until you KNOW that you can."

Nat looked up at her coach confused.

"Think back. Did you have any doubts about your ability before you tried that last dismount that caused your broken arm?" she encouraged Nat memory.

"Oh I don't know." Nat replied, "Wait! I do remember something. Do you think it could really have made a difference?" she asked her coach.

"Well, tell me what it is and I might be able to answer you better," her coach smiled down at her.

"Oh sorry, yeah I remember. I was watching some of the old Olympic gymnastic games and there was one girl who took a horrible fall in front of the whole world. She didn't break anything though."

"So how did that make you feel?" her coach encouraged her to go on.

"I remember saying to myself that I would NEVER do that to myself. Embarrass myself in front of the whole world like that. I remember seeing her face. It was bright red. Right after her routine she went off to the sidelines and tried to hide from the crowd. I could feel her embarrassment. It had been such a simple move and yet she had really messed it up. She'd ruined her shot. She would have had the gold." Nat remembered.

"Now think back to your fall. You were doing such an excellent job just before it happened, then you missed your mark. So what went through your mind in that moment? Can you remember?" Nat could feel that Mrs. Lovington was on to something.

"Yeah, I did the flip then bounced up for the finale and that picture of the girl in the Olympics falling flew into my mind. That's when I missed the mark and fell. WOW! I hadn't realized that. Do you really think that's why I broke my arm?" Nat was surprised at herself.

"You know, I wouldn't put it past it." Mrs. Lovington said. "So how can I get past this Coach?" Nat asked.

"Well, first you need to take on your part of the responsibility for your fall. You need to realize that it was a part of you who let you down, not just an accident. You let that image enter your mind. You could have ignored the feelings that went with it, but you didn't." she said.

"I can see that now. But I'm still so afraid to do it again. It hurt so much." Nat said. "Well, you know what?" her coach asked.

"What?"

"You have already had the worst that can happen. So now you have nothing to fear. You survived the worst, so it can only get better right?" she encouraged.

"I...I guess so." Natalie hesitated.

"Well, it's true. You need to DECIDE that you WILL achieve your goal, that you WILL get your gold medal." She continued, "Okay, we need to start over. Let's go over your goal again. We need to get you to a point where you can actually feel yourself winning the gold. You need to feel that wonderful moment in your heart when you land straight on your feet, your hands straight up in the air. You need to actually hear the crowd roar with their praise of your incredible routine. You need to feel their amazement surge through your entire body."

"Okay, I'll do that." Nat agreed.

"Are you willing to do whatever it takes to achieve your goal? Do you believe you will get that gold medal?" she encouraged.

"YES!" Nat affirmed.

"Good, then let's get started. We'll go over the whole routine again and again until it's solid in your subconscious. Then you will practice the routine diligently on the floor line that we use for practice until you have it absolutely perfect. Then, and only then, we will get you back up on the beam." Mrs. Lovington gave Natalie's shoulders a squeeze. Nat could feel the confidence and hope return to her body.

It was time. Nat tied the bandage on her lower arm tight, to give her the support she would need. She took in a deep breath, stood up and walked over to the beam. Mrs. Lovington was giving her a great big thumbs-up signal. She pushed the play button on the CD player to start the music for her routine. It was time. She had been practicing her routine on the floor line for almost a month now, and she had it down perfectly. She felt a quiver of doubt enter her mind and immediately pushed the thought away. She closed her eyes and imagined the roar of cheers that would come at the end of her routine. She could see it all, the judges, the other competitors, the dust still flying off the beam as she landed beautifully from her routine.

Another deep breath and she took a step forward, she was ready to run to the springboard to catapult herself up onto the beam and do her routine. The music rang out its starting tune. She could feel her body move all on its own. It felt natural. She KNEW in that moment as she ran onto the springboard, that she had already completed the routine beautifully, she just needed to finish her reality. Her confidence soared!

"You did it! That was absolutely your best routine ever! You're going to win the regional's, and you'll be winning that gold in no time. I'm so proud of you Nat." her coach beamed.

"I know it too, Coach" Nat smiled at her loyal coach. She knew she would get the gold medal. She had decided that it was hers. She really felt that it was hers already! She would never let fear get in her way again.

Activity 1

Questions from the story

- Whose fault was it that Nat broke her arm?
- What happened to Nat during her last dismount that caused her to break her arm?
- Which was stronger in Natalie after she broke her arm: Fear of being hurt, or, the Desire to win the gold medal?
- What exercises did Nat's coach, Mrs. Lovington, suggest to help Nat get her confidence up again?
- Where did Nat put her energy after her talk with Mrs. Lovington? Into her fear, or into her dream?
- How did Nat do on her routine after choosing to overcome her fear?
- Do you think Nat will get the gold medal? Why?

Useful questions to ask your child and write down together

- How have I given my power away?
- How will I handle fear when it comes up?
- What kind of help do I need to achieve my goals?
- How will I be when I have achieved my goals?

Activity 2

Take a quiet moment to sit down with your child and figure out what her biggest goal for her own future is. Have her write down all of her fears on one piece of paper and on another have her write down how she will feel the exact moment that she gets her goals. Then have her study both pieces of paper and have her decide which piece of paper she wants to put all of her energy into. Her energy is going to go into one of them regardless, so this is the chance for her to consciously decide which one to put her energy in. Then have her take her fear paper and rip it up into tiny pieces. Tell her to look at how she is bigger than her fear. She is able to rip it, not the other way around. Then have her take her other piece of paper, the one with how it will feel the moment she achieves her dream and have her place it next to her bed. Have her read it out loud to herself first thing in the morning and last thing before she goes to bed at night.

You can do this for yourself as well, show your child how important this activity is by role modeling it. She will feel a deeper connection to you for it.

Activity 3

Think back to your own life and share a story that relates to this topic, and discuss how you felt at their age, and what you learned from it.

"We have met the enemy, and he is us!"
-- From the comic strip Pogo *by Walt Kelly*

9 Forgiveness

> *"Forgiving is the pathway to happiness and the quickest way to undo suffering and pain."*
> *–Gerald Jampolsky, M.D.*

Forgiveness is so important. The biggest obstacle we have to getting the life we want is ourselves. Holding onto the past hurts and keeps us victims. Forgiveness is what allows us to move forward, past our own mental blocks. Forgiveness means to "give as before." This doesn't mean that your child should continue with a relationship with someone that may have hurt him. Often it's just the opposite. As long as he holds onto the pain from someone that hurt him, he is connected to that person. By releasing the resentment and the anger through the act of forgiveness, your child will be disconnecting from the pain that person may have caused him. This doesn't mean that your child is condoning the behavior of someone who hurt him; it's about him letting go of the need to blame and therefore, his need to suffer. It's not about forgiving others so much as it's about forgiving ourselves.

Your child may need to forgive others, but it doesn't have to do with the other people. It's actually all about your child. It's about how he feels. If he harbors anger from some past hurt, it hurts him to keep hanging onto it, and it will often show up in some physical illness in him. It could even become a disease. Disease means that your child's body is at "dis-ease" with itself. Forgiveness is about releasing the pain that he's kept inside of him.

The way to release is by expressing all of the feelings he has attached to it and then to finally accept that it happened, and that it is now over. That it does not deserve any more attention, once it has been finally thoroughly felt and released. It's time to move that negative energy into a more positive light, to help your child achieve his goals, and not keep holding back with the wounds of the past.

One technique to help your child release his feeling over his past situation is to do what we call the Soul Letter process. This is where your child will write his feelings down to express them. We've given you lead-in lines for your child to complete. Like "I'm so angry that..." Have your child give this a try. Don't worry if he doesn't know what he's feeling. This can help him sort out what's really inside of him. Often what we feel releases as we go through the writing process. You might want to make sure he'll have some tissues or a pillow nearby and after setting up the activity, give him the privacy he'll need to complete this activity. Have him use whatever works for him. Whatever he comes up with is okay. There are no wrong answers here.

If you see your child is overwhelmed to the point of an inability to function, or you feel you'd prefer to have someone personally guide your child, seek professional help from a licensed therapist or coach. If your child does see a professional, bring these Soul Letters along with him. If may serve to offer insight and speed to your child's healing process.

Okay, we've put the sections in the normal order that your child will feel the emotions. However, sometimes if your child is female, the first emotion she may feel will be sadness over anger. If you can see that she is feeling that more, then just start with the Sadness and Wounds section, then have her do the Blame and Upset section next. After that, have her continue as the remaining rest of the outline suggests. Remember it's important to encourage your child to express all of his emotions, and not to allow him to judge the emotions or himself, for that matter, as he goes through this process. Don't have your child edit, or worry about spelling or punctuation. Tell him he can even swear if he wants, and really encourage him to express himself fully. These letters are not to be shared*, they are just for your child! Let him know that you will not be reading them either. Have him make sure that he goes through the whole process, so he can complete the emotional release.

- These letters are not for sharing. These are intended to help your child heal and to help him connect to his Higher Self through Forgiveness.
- Your child may choose to share this letter, ONLY if the other person knows this process and agrees to share it, otherwise use it just for himself.
- ONLY share these letters with your child's licensed therapist or coach, if your child wants to. Otherwise don't insist.

Soul Letters can be used to help dump lots of emotional baggage. Your child may find that he will write these more to himself than to anyone else. The reason is that no one is as mad at your child, as he is with himself. Using the Soul Letters help your child to get rid of negative voices in his head; the ones that always say, "You can't," the ones that criticize him. It really works! Some other suggested recipients might be: you, his mom or dad, his sister, his brother, his teacher, his coach, his boss, his ex-girlfriend, or his ex-boyfriend, maybe his ex-best friend, etc.

Your child may have to write more than one of these letters to the same person. Don't have him try to solve a lifetime of his upset in one letter. Have him keep about two pages maximum per section, and encourage him to try to keep the sections relatively balanced. Remember, these are just for him. This will give him the freedom to express what he is really feeling, without having to live up to your or someone else's expectations. Make that clear to him.

Write each letter on a repeated topic or an individual event. In other words if the same behavior or argument with the same person occurs that is what the Soul Letter is about. Or if a particular event happened and he feels really upset about it; that is another subject of a Soul Letter.

Remember don't let him share them with the recipient. That often makes things worse. You may wish to encourage him to tear them up or even burn them to feel an additional release, or he can just hit his delete key!

One secret to doing this exercise – when someone may see what he's writing – is to have him only use the first letter of each word. It's gibberish to the average person, and he'll be able to write faster. It may be harder to re-read (if that's necessary for him), but he can write right in front of the person it's directed to without them knowing what he's up to! Have him try it! It really works!

---

*"Forgive us our trespasses,
as we forgive those who trespass against us."
– The Lord's Prayer*

Soul Letters: Seven Steps to Truth

Just fill in the lead in lines and keep repeating

until you feel a release,

then fully express your feelings.

Remember to have tissues and some pillows near, so if you feel the need to cry, or punch or scream into the pillows, you can without scaring the cat!

Blame and Upset

(Express all your feelings without judgment)

"I am so angry that….

It really upsets me when…"

Sadness and Wounds

"I'm really sad that… It hurt me when…"

Doubt and Fear

(This is the KEY level, this is what's really bothering your child)

"I don't know if… I'm afraid that…"

Responsibility and Guilt

(Here's where your child will dump his guilt for anything he's said, done, or not done)

"I'm sorry that I… I didn't mean to…"

Judgment and Forgiveness

"I forgive myself for believing myself as…"

"I forgive myself for believing as…"

Hopes and Wishes

(If your child could wave a magic wand, what would be the best thing he'd like to have happen regarding this issue?)

"I wish that… I really want to…"

Always add "This is something better for the highest good of all concerned."

Truth and Love

(Here's where your child will express his truth, love, appreciation and respect.)

"I love you for… I appreciate that…"

"I respect you for… The truth is…"

Story: Lucy Learns To Forgive

"No! Don't! STOP!" Lucy woke herself up from the terrible nightmare. Sally had been beating her up again under the bleachers. These dreams had been haunting Lucy all weekend ever since she had gotten the beating from Sally on Friday. She dreaded going back to school on Monday. She was embarrassed that she hadn't asked for help and she was terrified to hear Sally's tormenting.

"It's time to get up for school, honey!" her mom yelled up the stairs. "I'm not feeling well." She yelled back down again.

She could hear her mother's footsteps approach her door. Her mom knocked briefly and then let herself in when she heard Lucy's answer.

"Honey, you have to go. I know Friday was rough on you but you can't let your fear guide you. You have to face this head on. You need to forgive Sally and move forward." Her mom said.

"But Mom!" Lucy was sick and tired of hearing the same thing over and over again. Mom had been telling her to forgive Sally all weekend. It wasn't fair. Sally had been at fault, not her! But she was expected to make this go away. No one understood. She couldn't face Sally again. If Sally didn't torment her she was sure to beat her up again once she found out that Miss Jones knew about it. There was no way out.

"I'm sorry, honey, I can't let you stay home. You need to figure this one out and get past it. You can't continue to be afraid of her. You are attracting her vengeance and the sooner you realize that, and take on the responsibility then you will finally be able to face her again without any fear." Her mom insisted.

"You just don't get it!" Lucy was angry at her mom. She was angry at Sally for beating her up. She was angry at Miss Jones for telling her mom what happened. And she was angry at herself for not getting the help she should have gotten so she wouldn't have been beaten up in the first place. She was just down- right angry with everyone. It was a very dark place to be.

Grudgingly Lucy got herself dressed, ate her breakfast and then grabbed her books and ran out to catch her school bus. She sat by herself and didn't talk to anyone the whole way to school. She was sure she could hear the other kids snickering at her. When the bus got to the school, she sulked her way to her locker and put away her lunch and some of her books. Then she headed off to her first class.

After lunch Miss Jones asked Lucy to go to her office and wait for her. Lucy looked nervous. What had she done now? Was Miss Jones going to chew her out again for not having asked for help on Friday, when she could have avoided being beaten up by Sally? Lucy had not seen Sally today, which was odd. They always had French class together Monday mornings.

"Thank-you for coming here, Lucy," Miss Jones said as she walked into the room.

"Did I do anything wrong?" Lucy asked.

"No, not at all," Miss Jones smiled at her. "I wanted to talk about what happened on Friday. Friday didn't just happen out of the blue, did it?"

"I don't know what you mean." Lucy was confused.

Miss Jones explained, "Lucy, things happen to us in life because we attract them. Now I'm not saying that you asked Sally to beat you up." Miss Jones quickly added before Lucy could react. She continued, "What I would like you to think about is how you felt about Sally before it happened."

"I don't know." Lucy said.

"Were you afraid of her before this happened?" Miss Jones persisted. "Yeah, everyone is." Lucy replied.

"We have decided to expel Sally from our school. You are only one of many students who have been terrorized by Sally. We won't accept that kind of behavior here. I wanted to let you know that you don't need to worry about her anymore but I'm still worried about you Lucy." Miss Jones said quietly.

"I'm fine Miss Jones." Lucy replied.

"No Lucy, I can see that you are still very upset. I've been watching you all morning. I called your mother and she told me that you've been having constant nightmares. I'd like to do an exercise with you to help you get over this Lucy, if you're willing."

"What is it?" Lucy was curious. It would be great not to have the nightmares anymore.

Miss Jones had Lucy sit down and gave her a small pile of paper and a pen. "Okay, Lucy, I've written a few exercises for you to do on each paper. I want you to write out some Soul Letters."

"What's that?" Lucy asked.

"A Soul Letter is a letter that you write to your soul. You will write all about how Sally made you feel, how you made yourself feel, and so on. You'll see what I mean as you write these out. I've put the title and the opening sentences on each paper for you. I want you to feel safe knowing that no one will read these."

"Then why do it?" Lucy interrupted Miss Jones.

"This is an exercise for you. I feel confident that if you go through these exercises you will get past this, and the nightmares will stop. You'll be yourself again. You trust me right?" Miss Jones asked her.

"Of course I do." Lucy declared.

"Well, then trust me on this. Just do the exercises and then see how you feel afterwards, okay?" Miss Jones asked.

"Okay, Miss Jones, I'll do them." Miss Jones left her office and closed the door shut so Lucy would be all alone with the privacy she needed to do the exercises.

Lucy was curious. She turned over the first sheet, at the top it said, "This sheet is for all of your Blame and Upset." Then just a little further down she could see the first sentence had been started for her with the whole page left for her to fill in. It read, "I am so angry that… and It upset me when…"

Lucy took a deep breath and picking up the pen got ready to fill in the sheet. What was there to lose, if it didn't work she would be right back where she started.

She poured out her heart with all the anger and hurt that seemed to swell up on her mind. Her pen couldn't travel across the page fast enough. She flipped over the sheet and continued to fill it all up too. When she was done, she felt a little empty inside, kind of hollow. The anger and hurt were gone, but there was nothing else there either.

She reached for the second sheet. It was titled, "Sadness and Wounds" and it started with, "I'm really sad that... and It hurt me when..." And then just like the last one, the whole page had been left empty for her to fill. She took in another deep breath. She didn't know where to start. She still felt so empty inside. Then slowly the sadness rose within her and she found herself writing faster and faster. All of the sadness she had felt about being left out, about not having a close friend she could tell things to, and about so many other issues she had forgotten that seemed to come out of nowhere. She felt a quick moment of embarrassment, this was silly, what was she doing. But then it left and she continued to write.

The tears started to well up in her eyes. She reached out for the tissues on Miss Jones' desk. It was almost like she had left them there for her to use.

The next sheet read, "Doubt and Fear" at the top. Lucy immediately felt uncomfortable with this one. She didn't want to go back through all of her doubts and fears. But she knew she had to press onward and forward. So she took up her pen again and started to write next to the prewritten words, "I don't know if... and I'm afraid that..." Miss Jones had put a note at the bottom that read, "This is the KEY paper, this is what's really bothering you. Take your time with this one. Be completely honest with yourself."

It wasn't easy but slowly Lucy let herself go and opened up to her doubts and fears writing each one down as they showed their ugly heads. She felt ready to walk away from the exercise once she'd finished this last one.

There seemed to be no more of herself to give. But then the next paper's title caught her eye.

It read, "Responsibility and Guilt", this one was a shock. Wasn't this supposed to be about getting out the feelings she had about everything that had happened to her, not what she had done to others. Then as she lifted her pen to the beginning of the pre-written sentence, "I'm sorry that I... and I didn't mean to...," it came to her. She was sorry that she had treated herself so. She deserved better; and yet she had continually allowed bad things to happen to her. As she wept, she wrote down her deepest sorrow as she realized just how sorry she was for how she had treated herself. After she had filled the front with those feelings, she understood the guilt as well and filled up the entire backside with how guilty she had felt about everything that had happened to her. How she should have gone for help on Friday but hadn't, she felt guilty for having been so stupid to try to fix things all on her own. The page filled up from there.

She put the full paper aside and slowly grabbed the next. She felt so empty, so weak, she was sure that she couldn't go on. But she did. "Judgment and Forgiveness" she read. Forgiveness? Was she expected to forgive Sally for hurting her the way she had? How could she? Then a little note that Miss Jones had written in brackets caught her eye, "Forgiveness doesn't mean that you condone the behavior, it means that you accept that it happened, and that it is now in the past. You are willing to release the negative energy and move forward."

That she could understand. That she could do. There were two sections on the page; the first part began with, "I forgive myself for believing _____ as..."
She knew this one was meant to be about Sally. She wrote all about how she could release the bad feelings

that she had allowed Sally to give her. She was willing to let them go, to move on. It was incredible. She really felt that she could go on. She felt her energy return.

Then the second half said, "I forgive myself for believing myself as..." She immediately knew what she would write. She had thought she was weak, that she was not worth anything. She knew now that was not true, but she also knew that she could not be angry at herself for having believed that. Now was the time to forgive herself. To accept the fact that what she was, is no longer true. But it was what it was, and she accepted that. Now she could move on now from it.

Lucy gently laid the full paper aside. She wondered what on earth there was left to do, and yet there were still two more sheets to fill. She looked at the clock and was amazed. School was almost over. Where had the time gone? She knew she didn't need to worry about not showing up at her classes, Miss Jones' would have arranged all of that. As she thought it, there she was. Miss Jones poked in her head.

"Everything alright in here?" she asked.

"Just fine!" Lucy perked up, "I'm almost done, just two more pages to go," she said.

"Great! You'll really enjoy the next two. You still have forty-five minutes before your bus gets here, so you should have plenty of time. Just take it easy and enjoy. I'll make sure to come and get you before your bus arrives so you don't miss it. How are you feeling now?" Miss Jones enquired.

"Good, much better, these are great, thank-you." Miss Jones slipped away again and left Lucy alone to finish the last two pages.

The next one was titled, "Hopes and Wishes". "So that's why Miss Jones said I'd like these next two" Lucy smiled to herself. She was feeling much lighter and her energy was pouring back in.

Miss Jones had drawn the image of a magic wand on the top of the page with a small note that said,

"Imagine you could have anything you wanted to happen about this situation, what would it be? Dream BIG!" and she'd placed a little smiley face next to her note.

The sentence began, "I wish that…" This one was so much fun. She'd filled the first side within minutes. All of her hopes about how she would feel better about herself, and attract nice friends. Then she thought about wanting to deal with fear better, and knowing when to ask for help. The answers just seemed to pour out of her soul.

As she finished filling the second side of the paper she noticed the small note on the bottom of the page, it said, "This or something better for the highest good of all concerned." Lucy smiled. That was so true. Her wishes were not only for her but also for her family and also for Miss Jones. She wanted everyone to be happy. It was all for their highest good. She felt confident about her wishes. Sally was a distant memory now.

Finally she reached for her last sheet of paper, it said, "Truth and Love". It was broken into four sections, two on each side. The front two said, "I love you for…" and, "I appreciate that…" The back said, "I respect you for…" and, "The truth is…"

Lucy filled those two sides with all the love, appreciation, and respect she felt for her family, her teacher, Miss Jones and for herself. It felt great! When she finished and realized that she had a few minutes left, she even squeezed in a small section where she filled in all the love, appreciation and respect she had even for Sally. Yes, that's right. She had finally realized that it was because of how Sally had treated her that she was here right now, doing these exercises. She no longer hated her. She didn't really feel anything for her at all, except an appreciation for her having made the impression on her life. Because now she could grow and be stronger in her future. She was truly grateful for that.

The past was the past, but it helped her to be who she was right now, and she felt pretty happy with where she was right now.

"So how did you do? Did you manage to finish them all?" Miss Jones asked as she came back into the office, just as the end of classes bell rang through the halls.

"Yes! Here, look!" Lucy proudly held up her work.

"No, those are for you only. They are not meant for me. Did they help? You look much better." She observed.

"Yes, thank-you Miss Jones for making me do this. To be honest, at first I thought this was silly, I even had a moment when I felt embarrassed for doing it. But now, I'm really glad I stuck to it. I feel so much better!" Lucy beamed.

"I'm so pleased. Okay, off you go. Don't miss your bus. Take your sheets with you. You can take them home, read them over, and then destroy them. You don't want anyone to read these, they may not understand them and they may take them the wrong way. These were just tools to help you move on, they are no longer needed. You'll see that you will have them with you now, even after they're gone. Thank you for trusting me Lucy." Miss Jones said.

"Thank you Miss Jones. See you tomorrow!" she yelled over her shoulder as she raced to her locker to get her things. She felt better and the world looked brighter.

Activity 1

Questions from the story

- What was causing Lucy to have those nightmares?
- Why did Lucy not want to go to school Monday morning?
- Why did Miss Jones ask to see Lucy in her office?
- Why did Miss Jones want Lucy to fill in those seven pieces of paper?
- How did Lucy's attitude and energy change as she went through the process?
- Why did she have to forgive Sally?
- What does it mean to forgive?

Useful questions to ask your child and write down together

- What areas have I been stuck in?
- Who do I need to forgive?
- What do I need to forgive myself for?

Activity 2

Grab seven clean sheets of paper for your child. Write down one Soul Letter title on each paper:

Blame and Upset – "I am so angry that...It upsets me when..." (Feeling without judgment)

Sadness and Wounds – "I'm sad that... It hurt me when..."

Doubt and Fear – "I don't know if... I'm afraid that..." (This is KEY, what's really bothering you)

Responsibility and Guilt – "I'm sorry that I... I didn't mean to..." (Dump your guilt, anything you've said, done or not done)

Judgment and Forgiveness – "I forgive myself for believing myself as...I forgive myself for believing _____ as..."

Hopes and Wishes – "I wish that..." (This is where you get to have a 'magic wand', ask for what you would like to have happen from this situation. Remember to add this or something better for the highest good of all concerned.)

Truth and Love – "I love you for... I appreciate that... I respect you for... and The truth is..." (Express all your love, appreciation, respect and truth.)

Now have your child write out their own Soul Letters for each one, adding more paper wherever needed. Give them the space and privacy they need to complete these. It can be quite draining and also quite invigorating at the same time. Make sure they drink plenty of water and have a box of tissues or a pillow handy for them to really let themselves go. Don't ask to read what they write. This is for them to work out their own issues. Just be their coach. Then help them to destroy the papers after they are finished.

[Note: have them keep the letters if they will be seeing a therapist or coach and would like to share them]

Activity 3

Think back to your own life and share a story that relates to this topic, and discuss how you felt at their age, and what you learned from it.

---

*"Forgiveness is the answer to
the child's dream of a miracle,
by which what is broken is made whole again,
what is soiled is made clean again."
– Dag Hammarskjold*

---

10   Commitment

"Commitment is healthiest when it's not without doubt, but in spite of doubt."
– Rollo May PhD

Your child's commitment to herself is the key to making her change last. Commitment begins with deciding a goal that is S.M.A.R.T. Once your child has chosen her goals, make sure she writes them down, and have her verify that they meet all the S.M.A.R.T. criteria. Okay, now that your child knows where she wants to end up, she needs to go back from there, and determine what objectives she'll meet along the way to create the results she wants. Have her break them down into reasonably timed pieces. Your child will need to break them into monthly, weekly, and daily tasks, keeping the S.M.A.R.T. criteria in mind. Once she has her objectives broken down in small pieces, she will need to commit herself to doing them and to the specific action steps. Make sure you help your child build in guideposts of objectives needed to reach her goals to determine if she is on track.

Your child's commitment begins once she decides, really decides, something. What does it take to do that? How much does it mean to her? What if she was to look ten years down the road and nothing in her life had changed? How would that make her feel? How long will it take your child to do something different in her life? How long is she willing to wait? What if nothing has changed in five years? How will she feel then? Time moves quickly. This can sometimes be a difficult notion to pass on to your child, as for them time seems to move incredibly slowly at times. To help her get an idea, have her look back at her past. Have her look back two years. Point out how much she has already changed the past two years, and yet, it really is not all that long and yet she has grown so much in such a short time. Then have her look into her future again, and remind her that she will be that same two years older very soon. Does she want to stay with what she has now or does she want to finally commit to making a change? How long will she wait? If nothing changed in a year, what then? Is your child willing to take that chance? How long has it been since she knew she needed to a change? How much more time are you willing to wait for your child to change? Another month? Nothing changing? Another week? Another day? Another hour? Or can you help your child to change NOW? Commit NOW? Choose NOW? Decide you want something better in your child's life NOW! Don't wait. Make the decision to help your child shift her thinking NOW! Commit NOW! To quote the Nike shoe company slogan: "Just Do It." NOW! Commitment is powerful. It's a declaration to the world that you intend to do something.

Miracles happen with commitment.

Once your child is truly committed to herself and to her goals, she will achieve them, as long as she believes she can. If you find she needs help believing, just remind her of all the people who went before her. They created so much more than anyone would have ever believed. Landing a man on the moon began with a belief that we could. It began long before we knew how. It began with commitment.

On September 12, 1962, President John F. Kennedy stated, "We choose to go to the moon. We choose to go to the moon in this decade and do the other things, not because they are easy, but because they are hard, because that goal will serve to organize and measure the best of our energies and skills, because that challenge is one that we are willing to accept, one we are unwilling to postpone, and one that we intend to win, and the others, too." The President convinced others to believe with him, that it could be done. On July 20, 1969, when Astronaut Neil Armstrong took his, "One small step for man and one giant leap for mankind," that remark defined intention, belief and commitment.

Belief in yourself and belief in your goals is free. Why not chose to believe and choose to help your child to believe? Why not win in your own dream alongside your child? Are you ready to go for it? Is your child ready? Yes?

Great! Now that you and your child have committed to your goals, build support around you to help you to succeed. Find people you can depend on for positive support. Start with family or friends. Remember you want support, not ridicule for your child. Choose people you can depend on to believe with your child. Be her best support in her goals and dreams. Keep her accountable to them. If you would like some more support for you or your child, a helpful source can be found at http://www.getunstuck.com. You can also start your own Get Unstuck for Kids group!

"Life takes on meaning when you become motivated,
set goals and charge after them
in an unstoppable manner."
– Les Brown

Story:
Scottie Creates His First Vision Board

"Hi," as she burst in through the kitchen side door, "It sure smells good in here!" Suzy exclaimed to Scotties mom.

"Spice cookies." Scotties mom pointed to the oven as she continued, "Scottie's waiting up in his room. He sure is excited these last few days, what have you two been up to?"

"I'm just helping Scottie achieve his goals." Suzy said over her shoulder as she hung her thin jacket over one of the kitchen bench stools, and raced up to Scotties room.

"Hey Scottie, it's me," she said as she knocked briefly and slowly opened his bedroom door.

"Great, come in!" Scottie was happy to see her. He couldn't wait to hear about this next tool she was going to show him, to help him achieve his goals.

"So what's the next secret to the universe sending me my goals?" He waited no longer to ask.

"Okay, hold on, let me catch my breath. Alright, did you figure out what fears were holding you back from your goals?" Suzy asked.

"Yeah, I got that all sorted out, I made a list." Scottie handed Suzy his list of inner fears that had been holding him back from getting the things he wanted.

"Great work," Suzy commented. "Fantastic! Okay, now I'm going to show you the power of creating a vision board."

"A what?" Scottie looked like she was speaking a foreign language.

"A Vision Board. It's a board where you'll put up pictures of your dreams and positive affirmations to help your subconscious mind start to believe that your dreams are actually coming true. It's very powerful stuff, and it's really fun to do!" She said excitedly.

"What's an affirmation?" Scottie still didn't look sure.

"An Affirmation is a phrase or saying that assures your subconscious that a certain opinion about you is true. So for example what we are going to do tonight is go through your list of fears, and your 'perfect' day that you wrote a while back and then find photos and phrases that will show you these goals and fears in the positive." She said.

"Huh?" Scottie was getting more confused by the moment. "Why would I want to have photos of my fears on a board that I'm going to be looking at?"

"Sorry, I didn't mean to confuse you. Okay, let's go back a moment. Let's start with your goals. The ones you wrote about in your perfect day. Do you have that close by?" Suzy asked.

"Yeah, here it is," Scottie reached into his side table drawer and pulled out what looked like about four pieces of paper stapled together. He handed it to Suzy.

"Great, okay, first we'll go through this and just write down a simple list of the goals that you want to achieve.

Let's do that first. Then I'll tell you about the fear one. Okay?" she asked.

"Yeah, that sounds cool. I can do that." Scottie agreed.

After about ten minutes Scottie leaned back and put down his pencil and pad of paper. "That about does it. I can't think of another goal right now. I'll add more later, whenever I think of them, okay?"

"Sounds like a plan," Suzy smiled at him. "Okay, now we'll look over your fears. From your goals you can see that most of your goals have to do with what you want to have or what you want to do. Your fears will tell you what you want to be."

"You mean I want to be fearful? That's crazy!" Scottie chuckled. She knew he was only teasing, he realized by now that Suzy always had a hidden message; and he wanted to find out what this one was.

Suzy grabbed a pillow that was within reach and tossed it on top of Scotties head. "You monkey!" she laughed.

"No seriously, your fears will tell you what you really want to be. Here, let's take a look. Okay, see this top one?" she asked.

"Yeah," Scottie read it aloud, "I'm afraid of failing my grades this year. My grades have been really sliding down and I don't know why."

"Okay, now you know that you don't want to be afraid of failing your grades. What would be the opposite? What would you want instead?" Suzy asked him.

"I want to pass! Duh!" Now it was Scottie's turn to toss the pillow on Suzy's head.

Suzy chuckled, "You're sure a wise guy! No, come on be serious. Do you want to do this or not?"

"Okay, okay." He quieted down, "I want to pass with really great marks. I want to make my mom proud of me."

"Okay, that's it!" Suzy looked so excited that she looked like she was about to open a Christmas present. "What?" Scottie was thrown off.

"What you really want is to make your mom proud of you by getting good grades. It's not the grades so much as making your mom proud." She pointed out.

"Oh, yeah, I guess you're right. Yeah, I've been disappointing her so much lately. You think that's why my grades have been sliding?" he asked Suzy.

"Could be," she nodded. "Anyway, so that's one of the things to now add to your goal list, 'you make your mom proud' and 'you get great grades'. It's actually two things but they will work together. Okay, now let's go through the rest of your fears, and find out what your goals are for each one."

It took them another ten minutes before Suzy said, "Okay that was the last fear on your list. Let's start on your vision board. I have to go home soon, it's getting late, but I want you to see if you can find a happy picture to represent each goal from your photo browser on the internet, Okay?"

"Yeah, I can do that." Scottie agreed. He was looking forward to this part. It seemed like a lot of fun to go looking for photos of his dreams.

"Okay, when you're done, I want you to rewrite all of your goals in positive present tense. For example the one about getting your mom to be proud and to get great grades, write down something like: I always get the best marks in my class. I attract great pride from people like my mom consistently. Remember we cannot directly say that your mom will be proud, because that's intruding on her own free will, so instead you say someone like your mom, and then most likely in this case it will end up being your mom." Suzy smiled.

"Thanks Suzy, I really appreciate your help with all of this." Scottie said.

"No worries. It's fun, and I get to learn each time too. It's like a reminder for my own goals and dreams." She smiled. "Oh, one more thing before I go. I want you to pick one goal to work on first," and she left his room to head back home.

"So how did you do last night?" Suzy asked Scottie the next morning as they waited for their bus to school to arrive.

"Really great!" Scottie was still feeling that "high" that he had gotten from finding all those wonderful photos of his dreams.

"Good."

"Hey, what happened?" Suzy could see the depressed look on Scottie's face as he approached the bus on their way back home.

"Oh nothing, I guess it just takes some time. I flunked another math exam." Scottie said slowly. "Sorry to hear that but I'm glad to hear you saying, 'I guess it just takes some time'. That's a great attitude to have and it's true,"

Suzy beamed with delight. They stepped onto the bus as it slowed down to pick them up and take them home.

Sitting next to Scottie in the back seat Suzy continued, "Okay, so I'm guessing your first goal was to get great grades am I right?" she asked.

Scottie nodded his head.

"So my next question then is how committed are you to achieving that goal?" she looked hard at him. "What do you mean? I intended to do well today." He tossed back quickly.

"Did you?" Suzy interrogated, "did you study for it?"

"I was busy doing the goal thing. You said it was important." He replied.

"It is and I'll even go so far as to say that it is more important than your grades. This will help you for life. Once we grow up no one will really care if you flunked a test or not in high school. But this is not about the vision board. This is now about going for your goal. If you really want to do well then you need to commit to doing well. If you truly want to have the best grades that you can have so you can have that goal of seeing your mom smile when she sees your score, then you need to decide right now, that you will focus solely on this one goal, for right now, and take actions that will help you get this one done. Get it?" she asked him.

"Yeah, that makes sense. I guess I didn't really expect to do well today, I knew that I hadn't studied. I guess a part of me was hoping that this 'vision board' and 'perfect day' stuff would be kind of like magic. You know, the quick fix and all." He looked meekly at her and then gave her a slow wink.

"Scottie! This is serious business. If you really want to make a change in your life you need to Choose to behave differently, you need to fully commit to your goals. Get it?" she insisted.

"Okay, okay, I get it." Scottie said.

"So how did your test go?" Suzy asked Scottie as she got on the bus with him. It had been three weeks since he had first created his vision board and made his commitment to his first goal of getting great grades.

"A+!" he smiled.

"I knew you could do it." Suzy patted him on the back. "All thanks to you," he said back to her.

"Nope, all I did was send you in the right direction. But your success only came once you chose to fully commit yourself to your goals, and do what it took. So what's next on your list?" she asked him.

"To take you to the school dance," he said, "that is with 'someone like you'," he smiled cheekily at her. "Oh you!" Suzy reached over and swatted him playfully on his knee, "I'd love to."

If you want to create a digital vision board, check this out: http://www.mindmovies.com/index.php?10071

Activity 1

Questions from the story

- Why did Scottie need to have a look at his fears?
- How could he use his fears and turn them into goals?
- What happened on the first exam that Scottie took right after he created his vision board?
- Had he really committed to doing well on his exam?
- In what way was Scottie allowed to ask for pride from his mother for his goals, what words did his need to include, to make it so that he wouldn't violate her own intentions?
- What happened once Scottie really decided to commit to his goals sincerely?
- Who is Scottie's support?
- Why is it important for Scottie to keep hanging around with Suzy, how will it help him?

Useful questions to ask your child and write down together

- What are my S.M.A.R.T. goals for each area of my life?

- How can I get past what has stopped me from attaining goals in the past?

- What steps am I committing to taking?

- Who is in my support team?

Activity 2

Have your child go back over her own 'perfect day' and chose the most important goal for her to achieve first. Then have her commit, really commit to making it happen. Get her to tell you what her goal is if she is comfortable letting you know so that you can keep her accountable to her goal, just like Suzy keeps Scottie accountable to his goals. If your child doesn't feel comfortable telling you her goal, then ask her to share it with a good friend, a trusty relative, or a school teacher, someone who will want to truly keep her accountable to her goal, so that she doesn't let it slide back into the background of her mind. Show her by being a role model. Decide on a goal yourself, tell your child what it is, and ask her to keep you accountable. Lead by example.

Activity 3

Think back to your own life and share a story that relates to this topic, and discuss how you felt at their age, and what you learned from it.

"Do what you can, with what you have, where you are."
– Theodore Roosevelt

---

11 Gratitude

*"You don't know what you got till it's gone.
They paved paradise and put up a parking lot."
– Joni Mitchell*

Gratitude is something that changes how your child will feel about everything. Start him off by encouraging him to being grateful for what he already has. Watch how your child may begin to feel differently about what he has. Gratitude will help your child come from a place of having, vs. a place of lack. Too often we take what we have for granted. Recognition of the quality, value, significance, or magnitude of people and things is what true appreciation is.

Once your child learns to really appreciate everything he has, far beyond material possessions, real gratitude begins. He may start by appreciating each breath he takes, the warmth of the sun, the smile of a friend or the laugh of a child. Being consciously grateful will give your child a feeling of abundance and contribute to his sense of deserving.

Your child doesn't need to understand how gratitude works; he just needs to know it does. It's like a time I remember when I was a kid. My dad game me an allowance for doing chores. I spent it all in one day. I asked my dad for more. He said I'd have to learn to appreciate what I had first, before he'd give me anymore. That's how life works. Your child has to appreciate what he has, no matter what it is, before it gives him more.

I remember when I was first introduced to this concept. I started writing a gratitude journal every night before I went to bed. I committed to writing a minimum of three things I was grateful for. This was at a time in my life when I didn't really have much to be grateful for, and I sometimes struggled to find three things. Often my entries would be, "I'm grateful that I'm alive. I'm grateful I had something to eat today. I'm grateful it didn't rain today." Things started getting better.

Now I have much more to be grateful for, but it all began with the basics. I could go on and write many pages on what I am now grateful for, but what is more important is for your child to think about what he is grateful for. Have him think about what he has now. Get him to write a list of fifty things he's grateful for. For some people that might be easy, for others hard. Which will it be for your child? It's easy for your child to ask for more, but he first needs to realize what he already has – no matter how much that is – is a gift. He helped to create it, and he can help to create more.

I've had the chance to see others with more money and less happiness, and less money and more happiness. What does your child value most? If he has a roof over his head, food to eat, a safe place to sleep, and the ability to say what he wants, he is better off than ninety-five percent of the world. Instead of taking what he has for granted, your child needs to learn to appreciate everything he does have. It's easy to get caught up in the, "look what someone else has compared to me," syndrome. Remind your child that we only 'rent' everything on this planet. Except for love, your child can't take any of his things with him. Does he appreciate the people in his life?

Often your child may not realize what he has until it's taken away. That's a hard way to learn how to be grateful. Unfortunately, that's how some of us must learn. Worse yet, sometimes that's when your child doesn't feel grateful at all. How he faces change is up to him. You can coach and encourage him but in the end it's still up to him to change. It's a choice that can change his life in a positive way if he wants it to.

It's up to him. Encourage him to just do it.

"No one is as capable of gratitude as one who has emerged from the kingdom of night."
– Elie Wiesel

Story: Jessie Learns About Gratitude

"10 Bucks! Is that ALL?" Jessie was outraged. Her best friend, Sonia got at least $20 bucks each week for her allowance. "Mom, I've got to get more than that! None of the kids in school get anything less than a 20!"

Mrs. Johnson took a deep calming breath, reached out, grabbed the $10 dollar note and said, "Okay Jessie, if you don't want that, then I'll take it back. You can go find a way to make your own money. I'm not going to give into these silly games about how much your friends get. Once you grow up you won't be making the same money as them either. Everyone gets a different amount of things in life. Now is as good a time as any for you to figure that one out. And you can begin by realizing all that you have to be grateful for."

She put the $10 back in her wallet, turned on her heel and walked away.

Jessie's mouth was getting dry. It was still hanging open from the shock. She hadn't expected her mom to take the money back.

"Mom, wait!" She chased her mom into the kitchen, "Wait mom, I'm sorry, I didn't mean to be ungrateful, I'll be happy with the $10. Please mom, give it back to me. I won't ask for more, I promise," she begged.

"No, I'm sorry Jessie, it's too late. I am stopping your allowance altogether until you find the true meaning of gratitude." Jessie's mom grabbed the laundry basket on the bench top and walked back to the laundry room to collect the wet clothes to hang outside.

It was no use. Jessie knew her mom well. Whenever her mom decided something, she stuck to it. It wasn't fair! She was sure it was a violation of child rights!

She ran up to her room and banged her door shut. She'd show her mom about gratitude alright! Her mom just didn't appreciate all the things she did for her. It was plain child labor, that's what it was!

Jessie ranted and raved out loud about all the horrible things she was forced to do for her mom, like washing the dishes every night, making her bed and keeping her room tidy, and she even had to sort her own laundry, not to mention clean her own bathroom! It just wasn't fair. And now she wouldn't even be paid for it anymore! She was going to ring up the council and report her mom about child labor, that's what!

Rrrrring!

Jessie was thrown out of her self-pity moment to the sound of her private phone ringing impatiently off the hook. She picked it up and answered, "Yeah, hello, house of child-slave Jessie reporting."

"Jessie, is that you? What do you mean child-slave? What's up?" it was Sonia on the other end.

"Oh Sonia, you won't believe it! Mom took away my allowance!" she sobbed into the phone. "Oh Jessie, how horrible! WOW, what happened?" she asked.

"Nothing! I just asked for a few more dollars and WHAM, she stole my money, grabbed it right out of my hand and put back in her wallet, and now she says she won't pay me ANY allowance money! Get that!" Jessie wailed.

"Wow, I think that's illegal!" Sonia supported her friend.

"I know! I'm going to the council building tomorrow and I'm going to find out about it! I'm going to set this right, that's for sure. She's not going to get away with it!" Jessie replied.

They talked for at least an hour, complaining back and forth to each other about how unfair life was and how hard it was, having to do homework and stupid chores and all that child labor stuff.

After school the next day, Jessie and Sonia walked downtown to the council building. They entered and walked up to the receptionist.

"Excuse me, where do I go to complain about family violations against child labor?" Jessie asked.

"You'll want counter number 6 at the end. Just take a number and they'll let you know when it's your turn." She replied, not responding at all to the plea about child labor. She just sat there playing a computer game and chewing her gum with her mouth wide open. Jessie and Sonia heard her crack a bubble as they took their seats close to counter 6 after grabbing a number ticket.

"Wow, there sure are a lot of people here!" Sonia looked around. There were at least twenty people ahead of them in line.

"This is going to take a while." Jessie sighed, "But I'm not giving up, this is important, it's about violating a child's rights!" she determined.

A little girl about four years old asked her mom across the aisle from Jessie, "Momma, what's a child's right?".

"It means the government gives little girls like you the right to be safe and protected from bad things." Her mother answered her.

"Like Daddy?" the little girl asked her mother.

"Yeah, like Daddy," her mother answered her gently.

"Then why do they make me have to go see him?" the little girl continued to ask. "Oh sweetheart, I know, it's not fair is it?" her mother answered her.

"But Mommy, he's really mean, he scares me Mommy. Last time he got so angry, his faced was all red and puffy! Mommy, He yelled at me and grabbed me really hard on my arm." The little girl started to lift the sleeve of her top to show her mommy. Both Jessie and Sonia caught a glimpse of the huge dark blue bruise before the little girl's mom quickly pushed her sleeve down again to hide it.

"But why Mommy? Why do I HAVE to see him?" she insisted.

"Oh Honey, I wish I knew, I'm hoping they'll give us a court order today saying that you won't ever have to see him again." Her mother answered her gently.

"I hope so." The little girl said back, wise beyond her years.

"Mrs. Smite, you and your little girl may come in now." The receptionist at counter 6 said. The little girl and mother stood up and walked to the counter and entered the side door. "Wow, did you see that?" Sonia asked Jessie in awe.

"Yeah, that must have hurt bad! What a brave little girl." Jessie answered. "He should be sent to jail!" Sonia said with determination.

"Yeah," was Jessie's only reply. Seeing that poor little girl had made her feel very uncomfortable inside. That girl really didn't have her rights protected. Jessie's mom would certainly never hurt her. She couldn't remember even one time when her mom hit her. They just didn't do that in their house. Jessie couldn't believe that there were parents out there that would do such a horrible thing. How could they?

Jessie and Sonia sat quietly for another 10 minutes.

The door opened again next to counter number 6 and the little girl and mother walked out. The little girl was crying.

"But I don't wanna see Daddy!" she wailed.

"I know honey, I know." Her mother tried to console her. "But Mommy, he hurts me!" she kept on crying.

"I'm so sorry honey." The little girl's mother bent down and scooped her daughter up into her arms and carried her out of the office. Jessie could see that the mother was crying too.

"Next, number 146 please." The receptionist said out loud.

"That's us Jessie." Sonia poked Jessie in the arm and stood up to go.

"Wait." Jessie took one more long look outside the glass doors at the poor little girl in her mother's arms, crossing the parking lot. "I want to go home now."

"But it's our turn," Sonia pleaded.

"I can't do it Sonia. Mom may have been hard on me to take away my allowance but she's never, and will never hurt me like that little girl's daddy did. I can't complain about her now." Guilt at having even thought about filing a complaint against her mother bathed her cheeks in red fire.

"Sorry, Miss, I'll pass." Jessie said to the receptionist.

"Next, number 147 please." The receptionist said like a robot.

"Let's go home." Jessie turned to Sonia. "I'll find my own way to make money. Dad's always coming up with money making ideas for kids all the time. I'll just try one of those."

"Huh?" Sonia was still in a daze.

"Come on, I want to go home." Jessie ran out the door.

"Mom? Where are you Mom?" Jessie raced into the house shouting.

"I'm in here," she heard her mother say from Jessie's bedroom upstairs. Jessie raced up the stairs missing every second step. Jessie found her mom making up Jessie's bed with fresh, clean sheets. A tear came to Jessie's eye. She wiped it away, ran to her mom, and surprised her with a great big bear hug saying, "Thank-you Mom, I love you!"

"Where did that come from?" her mom was taken off guard.

"Nothing Mom, I just finally realized how much you do for me. I'm sorry I've been so spoiled. I know now why you took away my allowance…"

"I'm not going to give it back to you, if that's what you're trying." Her mom interrupted her.

"No Mom, I don't want you to. I'm going to try one of Dad's ideas and make my own money. I'm just sorry I was so rude to you. Thanks Mom, I love you!" Jessie hugged her again, and then ran downstairs to figure out how she was going to make her own money. She knew she would make her mom and dad proud.

Upstairs, her mom sat down on Jessie's bed and said, "Well, I'll be darned, I think she really got it!"

Activity 1

Questions from the story

- What did Jessie's mom do to Jessie that made Jessie so mad?
- What was Jessie going to do to get back at her mom?
- Why did Jessie change her mind about complaining to the authorities about her mom?
- Do you think the authorities would have done anything anyway?
- How did watching the little girl change how Jessie felt about her own life?
- Do you think Jessie fully realized how blessed she was in her own life?
- How did Jessie show her mom her gratitude immediately?
- How else was Jessie planning to show both her parents her extreme gratitude?

Useful questions to ask your child and write down together

- What things do I have to be grateful for daily and why?

- Who am I grateful to have in my life, and why?

- What things about me am I grateful for?

Activity 2

Create a Gratitude Journal with your child. Get a notebook and have your child decorate it so that it looks really special; maybe with glitter, stickers, stamps or some other decorations. Title it, "My Daily Gratitude Journal". Then have your child write the date on the top of each entry and write down three things they are grateful for each day. It can be as simple as, "I'm grateful for the yummy toast I had this morning for breakfast." It's not important so much what they are grateful for as to the mindset that this exercise will create for your child. Now set an example and create your own Gratitude Journal. Maybe set up a special time of day when you both write in your Journals. You don't need to share your entries, just the positive energies. Then whenever you or your child is not feeling grateful, refer back to the journal, and you will remember gratitude!

Activity 3

Think back to your own life and share a story that relates to this topic, and discuss how you felt at their age, and what you learned from it.

"Gratitude is not only the greatest of virtues, but the parent of all others."
- Cicero

---

12   Your Child's Next Step

*"They always say time changes things,
but you actually have to change them yourself."*
– Andy Warhol

Moving forward in your life can be scary for your child, because doing so will take her out of her comfort zone. If after she begins to make some positive changes and feels uncomfortable or feels fear coming up, that's great! This means she is stepping out of her comfort zone, and changing patterns, which will allow her to change what she has in her life. Keep on coaching and encouraging her to take these scary steps because everything that she wants but doesn't yet have is outside of her present comfort zone.

Getting your child to trust herself and the process, while believing she can attain what she desires, is all that she needs. Growth doesn't always feel pleasant, but the outcome will lead to positive results. Little steps at first are all that are required.

Here are some suggestions to get your child started:

- Have your child begin with writing something in her "gratitude journal" each night. Have her write three things that she is grateful for.
- Get your child to take five minutes each morning to sit and be quiet, listening to her inner wisdom. If she finds she is getting a consistent message,

encourage her to follow through on it. See what happens.

- You child should take five minutes to appreciate someone in her life.

- Take your child on a walk in nature, noticing everything that surrounds her.

- Encourage your child to begin journaling. Have her write down her feelings and thoughts at least four times a week. This will be private, for her eyes only. Get her to watch for patterns that emerge in her journaling. The simple act of "paying attention" may help your child to notice what's been in front of her for years. She may be surprised to find how simple it can be to find what she needs to change and create.

- Get your child to write down what she wants to create in her life. Have her write out her S.M.A.R.T. goals, and create a plan to achieve these goals. She can then break her plan into daily, weekly, and monthly action steps. You can help her with these, and hold your child accountable to her goals. Have your child build in guideposts to let her know if she's still on track. Have her make adjustment as needed. Let her be open to fine tuning her goals along the way.

- She can let go of the goals that no longer fit, and create new ones as her perception about life shifts.

- Make sure your child keeps balance in her life. She needs to feed her emotional, spiritual, mental and physical sides to reach her weekly goals.

- Be sure that she is true to herself. She must learn to love and accept herself. She needs to learn to love and accept others. You can help by being her role model, showing her how you fully accept yourself as you are, and how you fully accept others as they are. Teach her to love life by loving life yourself.

- Build a support team of positive loving people for your child. Have her also build in rewards along the way.

Congratulations on making it through this book. You have already taken positive steps towards changing your child's life. Remember...never underestimate the power of your thoughts to create new possibilities! As you follow the suggestions in this book, you will find much of the clarity you have been seeking for your child. The stories that are attached to each chapter are there as tools to help you pass along the many messages that are sometimes otherwise so hard to pass on to your child. You have all the tools you need inside YOU! Don't forget how powerful role modeling is for your child. You also have the ability to make changes in your life to begin creating the life you really want as does your child.

Share this with others. You may find helping other parents will help you as well and may be a great way to create the support that you need.

You have gone from a feeling of being stuck, not knowing how to help your child, to knowing how you can help your child to want to change her life. You have an understanding of what you can do to move your child forward and make positive changes in both your lives. You have found ways to help your child take her power back by developing new habits of keeping her word. You now have tools for helping your child create the life that she truly desires through focus, forgiveness and gratitude.

Finally, you have committed to helping your child make new choices, and to demonstrate gratitude for what she already has. Remember, YOU are courageous, as is your child. Reach for YOUR dreams too, as you help your child reach for hers. Believe it is possible to create the life you both are dreaming of and MORE!

This book is a tool. Use it as a reference guide, over and over, to free you and your child up whenever either one of you gets "stuck" in your life. Read the stories in this book to your child over and over, until their messages are deeply ingrained into her soul. Make the learning fun, giggle, laugh, discuss the characters and the choices they make and how they would be if they had made them differently. Keep this book with you, and reference it anytime you're feeling the need to change. We hope it will bring you to the place you want yourself and your child to be in your lives. Take the action steps that make sense to you. Be gentle with your child and yourself as you go through this process. Make your lives what you really want them to be! Believe you both can do it!

You can!

"When you're at the end of your rope, all you have to do is make one foot move out in front of the other. Just take the next step. That's all there is to it."
– Samuel Fuller and Milton Sperling

Story: Scottie Finally Gets What He Wants

"I just feel so overwhelmed, Suzy, I don't know where to begin!" Scottie moaned. He was feeling quite desperate.

Suzy reached over and touched his hand, "How would you eat an elephant?" she smiled. "What?" Scottie was thrown out of his misery.

"How would you eat an elephant?" Suzy repeated.

"A whole elephant? Are you kidding? I could never do that." Scottie was flabbergasted. "One bite at a time!" Suzy calmly said as she stroked his knee lovingly.

"One bite at a time. I get it!" Scottie nodded to himself under his breath. He turned to her and bent forward and gave Suzy a soft kiss on her lips. "Thank-you Suzy," he said.

Activity 1

Questions from the story

- What did Suzy mean?
- Why did Scottie feel better after he figured out he could eat a whole elephant "one bite at a time"?

Useful questions to ask your child and write down together

- What can I do today to move me toward my goals?
- What information do I need to know to begin?
- How much do I want this, and what am I willing to do to change?
- What is my first step to do to take action now?

Activity 2

This is it! It's time to sit down with your child and make a plan. First write out your goals, do it together, be a team. Have two pieces of paper, one for your child and one for you. Mastermind, figure out your family goals and your individual goals. Then list the goals and place a letter beside each goal, don't worry about the order of importance.

Then draw this line on a second piece of paper. Do this for both of you.

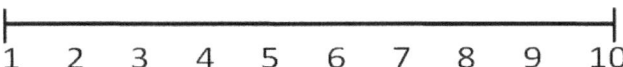

Now take your list of goals with the letter allotted to each and place your goals on this line in the order of their importance to you. 1 being "not so important," and 10 being "of high importance." After you place your goals on the line then take all of the ones that make a placement of an 8 or higher and work on these ones first. Accomplish these first. The more you want a goal the more likely you'll be to achieve it. After you have achieved these goals, only then go back and work your way down your list, adding new ones as new goals pop up and scratch out ones that are no longer important to you.

Here' what it might look like:

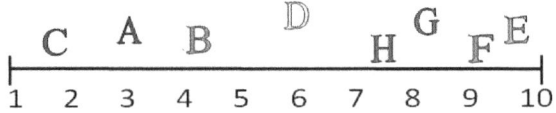

In this case G F & E would be your first goals to work on.

Activity 3

Think back to your own life and share a story that relates to this topic, and discuss how you felt at their age, and what you learned from it.

"Every journey begins with a single step."
– Ancient Chinese Wisdom

Other Titles by John & Amanda

John Seeley M. A.

Get Unstuck! The Simple Guide to Restart Your Life

Get Unstuck! The Simple Guide to Restart Your Life, Audiobook

Get Unstuck! The Workbook

Liberate! La Guia Sencilla Para Reiniciar Tu Vida

Keep On Believing, Stories of Inspiration, Courage and Triumph

Get Unstuck in Relationships! Coming soon!

Get Unstuck in Business! Coming soon!

Available for Speaking & Interviews

http://www.johnseeleyma.com/engage.php

http://www.johnseeleyma.com/presskit.php

www.keeponbelieving.com

Amanda van der Gulik

The Insider's Secrets to Teaching Children About Money

Allowance Secrets: To Give Or Not To Give?

The Cleverville Challenge

50 Easy Ways for Kids To Make Money

Why Every Child Should Have 6 Piggy Banks

Available for Speaking

www.AllowanceSecrets.com

www.GetUnstuckForKids.com

Resource Suggestions

www.johnseeleyma.com/membership

http://johnseeleyma.com/blog/

www.johnseeleyma.com/products.php

http://tinyurl.com/unblocksuccess

Click Here to Get a Free 30 min. coaching session

http://www.johnseeleyma.com/coach.php

www.ingramcontent.com/pod-product-compliance
Lightning Source LLC
Chambersburg PA
CBHW061759110426
42742CB00012BB/2182